Gary
Paulsen

The People to Know Series

Madeleine Albright
*First Woman
Secretary of State*
0-7660-1143-7

Neil Armstrong
*The First Man
on the Moon*
0-89490-828-6

Isaac Asimov
*Master of
Science Fiction*
0-7660-1031-7

Robert Ballard
*Oceanographer Who
Discovered the* Titanic
0-7660-1147-X

Willa Cather
Writer of the Prairie
0-89490-980-0

Bill Clinton
*United States
President*
0-89490-437-X

Hillary Rodham Clinton
Activist First Lady
0-89490-583-X

Bill Cosby
Actor and Comedian
0-89490-548-1

Walt Disney
*Creator of
Mickey Mouse*
0-89490-694-1

Bob Dole
Legendary Senator
0-89490-825-1

Marian Wright Edelman
*Fighting for
Children's Rights*
0-89490-623-2

Bill Gates
*Billionaire
Computer Genius*
0-89490-824-3

Jane Goodall
Protector of Chimpanzees
0-89490-827-8

Al Gore
*Leader for the
New Millennium*
0-7660-1232-8

Tipper Gore
*Activist, Author,
Photographer*
0-7660-1142-9

Ernest Hemingway
Writer and Adventurer
0-89490-979-7

Ron Howard
*Child Star &
Hollywood Director*
0-89490-981-9

John F. Kennedy
*President of the
New Frontier*
0-89490-693-3

Stephen King
*King of Thrillers
and Horror*
0-7660-1233-6

John Lennon
The Beatles and Beyond
0-89490-702-6

Maya Lin
Architect and Artist
0-89490-499-X

Jack London
*A Writer's
Adventurous Life*
0-7660-1144-5

Barbara McClintock
*Nobel Prize
Geneticist*
0-89490-983-5

Rosie O'Donnell
*Talk Show Host
and Comedian*
0-7660-1148-8

Christopher Reeve
*Hollywood's Man
of Courage*
0-7660-1149-6

Ann Richards
*Politician, Feminist,
Survivor*
0-89490-497-3

Sally Ride
*First American Woman
in Space*
0-89490-829-4

Will Rogers
Cowboy Philosopher
0-89490-695-X

Franklin D. Roosevelt
*The Four-Term
President*
0-89490-696-8

Steven Spielberg
Hollywood Filmmaker
0-89490-697-6

John Steinbeck
America's Author
0-7660-1150-X

Martha Stewart
*Successful
Businesswoman*
0-89490-984-3

Amy Tan
*Author of
The Joy Luck Club*
0-89490-699-2

Alice Walker
*Author of
The Color Purple*
0-89490-620-8

Simon Wiesenthal
*Tracking Down
Nazi Criminals*
0-89490-830-8

Frank Lloyd Wright
Visionary Architect
0-7660-1032-5

People to Know

Gary Paulsen

Author and Wilderness Adventurer

Edith Hope Fine

Enslow Publishers, Inc.

40 Industrial Road	PO Box 38
Box 398	Aldershot
Berkeley Heights, NJ 07922	Hants GU12 6BP
USA	UK

http://www.enslow.com

For Donna, Jodie, Judith, Hilary, Karen, Kathleen,
Marie, Nina, Stephanie, and Suzan.
They know why.

Library of Congress Cataloging-in-Publication Data

Fine, Edith Hope.
    Gary Paulsen : author and wilderness adventurer / Edith Hope Fine.
        p.   cm. — (People to know)
    Includes bibliographical references and index.
    Summary: A biography of the outdoor adventurer and author, whose writing
includes adventure stories, historical novels, sports books, and nature stories.
    ISBN 0-7660-1146-1
    1. Paulsen, Gary—Juvenile literature. 2. Authors, American—20th century
Biography—Juvenile literature. 3. Adventure and adventurers—United States
Biography—Juvenile literature. 4. Wilderness areas—Juvenile literature. [1.
Paulsen, Gary. 2. Authors, American.] I. Title. II. Series.
PS3566.A834Z66   2000
813'.54—dc21
[B]   99-37950
                                                  CIP

Printed in the United States of America

10 9 8 7 6 5 4 3

To Our Readers:
All Internet addresses in this book were active and appropriate when we went to press.
Any comments or suggestions can be sent by e-mail to Comments@enslow.com or to
the address on the back cover.

Illustration Credits: © 1999 *Star Tribune*/Minneapolis-St. Paul, pp. 79, 83;
C. Mitchell, courtesy of Flannery Literary, pp. 88, 101; © Corel Corporation,
p. 10; Courtesy of Delacorte Press, Random House Children's Book Group,
p. 96; Courtesy of Flannery Literary, pp. 15, 24, 28, 37, 108; Dave Monson,
p. 70; Edith Fine, pp. 11, 56, 104; Enslow Publishers, Inc., p. 98; Greg Fine
illustrations, pp. 46, 64, 70; Jeff Ruppenthal, *The Daily News*, Lebanon, PA,
courtesy of Hershey Middle School, p. 76; Minnesota Historical Society,
p. 32; Reprinted with permission of the *Duluth News-Tribune*, Minnesota,
p. 73; Rick Schrock, courtesy of Flannery Literary, p. 93; Ruth Wright
Paulsen, courtesy of Flannery Literary, pp. 8, 55, 59, 67; U.S. Department of
the Interior Bureau of Land Management, p. 64.

Cover Illustration: John Schnack Pictures

Contents

Acknowledgments

What joy for a bibliophile to read a body of work in the name of "research."

Many people have helped with this project. To all of them, my thanks:

Penny Sue Arnold, Hershey Middle School, Hershey, Pennsylvania

Patricia Hatfield, Carlsbad City Library, Carlsbad, California

Hilary Crain, Dieguño Junior High School, Encinitas, California

Janelle and Michael Fine

Greg Fine

Abby Williams Gese and Jennifer Flannery, Flannery Literary

Koochiching Historical Society, Koochiching, Minnesota

Wendy Lamb, Delacorte Press, Random House Children's Book Group

Minnesota Historical Society, St. Paul, Minnesota

Jodie Shull, Palomar College

Theodore Taylor

A Mystical Run

"If I hung a right, I could stay in the beauty."[1]

On a glistening clear night in northern Minnesota, Gary Paulsen and his dog team glided through the piercing cold. Under a full moon, they raced across the frozen ice of Clearwater Lake about midnight, then started up a hill. Moonlight shone down on him and the team. As they passed through a stand of great Norway pines, it seemed to Paulsen like a cathedral.[2]

"When dogs run, they're absolutely silent," said Gary Paulsen, a master storyteller. "They never make a sound . . . and all the steam from their breath came over their backs and hit me. And it was like I was being pulled by a silent steam ghost up through the moonlight."[3]

As they crested the hill, Paulsen saw a scene of

Gary Paulsen, with his dog Sheba

heart-stopping beauty. Deep inside, he felt a pull. There in the stillness Paulsen had a choice. He could turn the sled left and ride nineteen miles back to home and safety—his wife and son, food and warmth—within a few hours. Or he could follow the light, letting feelings and wonder draw him.

Gary Paulsen did what he had done many times in his life. He chose the unknown.

For eight days and nights, he ran with the dogs.

"I went all over," said Paulsen. "I think I crossed into Canada . . . I had a wonderful time."[4] In the exhilaration and solitude of those eight days, he learned more about himself than many people learn in a lifetime.

Sure that her husband had fallen through the ice, Ruth Paulsen alerted searchers. They combed the woods for Gary and his dogs. When he returned home, she knew at once that he had been changed.

Even after he returned, the startling beauty, the bone-deep cold, the bond with his beloved dogs, and the silence were his forever. Like a young animal, he had been imprinted by the natural world. His life would never be the same.

This solitary run through time and snow would lead Paulsen to tackle the Iditarod, the grueling 1,049-mile run through the wilds of Alaska. In awe of his dogs and in love with sledding, Gary Paulsen would run the race not once, but twice.

In the time Paulsen might call simply *Before*, he had been a farmhand, ranch hand, soldier, actor, singer, director, truck driver, sailor, teacher, editor, migrant farmworker, sailor, animal trapper, field engineer,

"When dogs run, they're absolutely silent," says Gary Paulsen.

and professional archer. He had also written more than thirty books.

In *After*, the time following his deeply felt, transforming run, he was a different person. New. Paulsen would continue to draw on his past life with its rough-and-tumble childhood, wild adventures, and snap decisions, but sledding and dogs would drive his work many times.

For his books, Gary Paulsen draws deeply on his own experiences, layering them with intriguing plots. He becomes his characters, knows their feelings and secrets, senses their problems. With enticing simplicity and rhythm, Paulsen's words reach out from the page like a hand to grab readers and pull them into his tales.

Students devour Paulsen's books. From the rollicking *Harris and Me* to the phenomenally popular *Hatchet*, from the searching *Canyons* to the poetic *A Christmas Sonata*, Paulsen's books fly off the shelves.

"In the library," said one young reader, "you don't want to say you've found one of [Gary Paulsen's] books because if it's in your hand, someone will come and grab it and everyone will be fighting for it."[5]

Gary Paulsen writes about his life. If he has thrown a stick at a bear, nearly drowned, been blown

As an author, Paulsen draws on his adventures and experiences.

off a mountainside or chased by a moose, he has written about it.

Today, with more than two hundred books to his credit, Paulsen is a writing machine. His focused themes and riveting styles make for spellbinding reading. Fans pester him for more. They flood him with mail. They tell him that he is the reason they read.

Young people count on Gary Paulsen to tell each story with the edginess and uncertainty of real life. His words ring true, zinging straight to his readers' minds and hearts.

Childhood: At Home and Abroad

"She didn't think I remembered . . . but I had. I remembered it all."[1]

Gary Paulsen lived the first seven years of his life with his mother, Eunice Paulsen. His father, Oscar Paulsen, an Army officer, was absent. When Gary was born in Minneapolis, Minnesota, on May 17, 1939, his father was overseas, stationed with General George Patton in Europe during World War II. Eunice Paulsen kept a framed snapshot of her husband, often reminding Gary that the man in the Army uniform was his father.

Even when he was a small boy, Gary's mind could record events with the clarity of a video camera. This almost photographic memory would later serve him well as a writer.

One Christmastime, when Gary was four, he went by train with his mother to visit an aunt and uncle at

Rainy Lake, on the northern border of Minnesota. There he met his cousin Raleigh, who was very ill. Raleigh's parents—Gary's aunt and uncle—knew this would be their child's last Christmas. As a gift of love for their dying child, they engineered a magical memory.

Late Christmas Eve, the boys heard bells. Outside in the snow appeared a sleigh pulled by four reindeer. In the sleigh was Santa Claus.

Four-year-old Gary decided to test whether Santa was real. He put out his hand and touched one of the reindeer. Then he bravely reached up and tugged at Santa's beard. Both the reindeer and the beard were real. Paulsen's book *A Christmas Sonata* gently captures his memories of those true events.

Gary spent much of his early childhood in Chicago. Starting in early 1944, his mother worked the swing shift, from late afternoon until midnight, in a plant that manufactured ammunition for the military. Gary's baby-sitter was an old woman named Clara, who drank red wine from a jelly jar. She paid so little attention to Gary that he did not even know whether she liked him or not.

Clara and Gary would sit together and listen to the evening shows on the radio. Sometimes she talked back to comedian Red Skelton as he acted out characters like Clem Cadiddlehopper. Sometimes she yelled at Mortimer Snerd or Charlie McCarthy, the wooden dummies of ventriloquist Edgar Bergen. Young Gary took in Clara's strong language, then carefully practiced swearing.

Gary had just turned five when he found himself

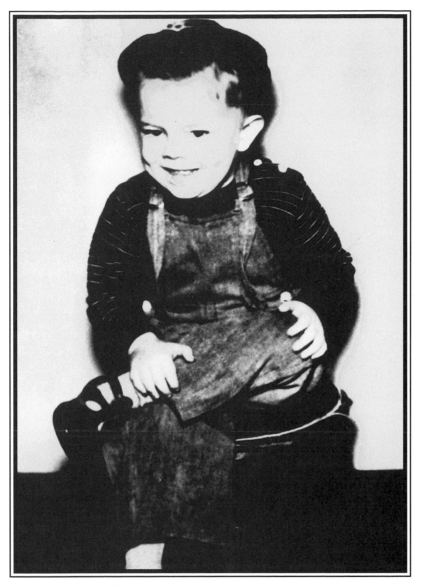

Gary was about three years old when this photo was taken to send to his father, who was overseas during World War II.

on another adventure. Trusting kind railroad porters, his mother pinned a note to his jacket and sent him to be with his grandmother. The long train ride took Gary to a cookcamp west of International Falls, Minnesota. Alida Moen, Eunice Paulsen's mother, worked there as a cook for a crew building a road into Canada.

Gary was enchanted, caught up in the wonder of this new world. For him, the workers were like huge, gentle bears. He sat on their laps in the great machines, working the levers, his small hands covered by their large ones.

The young boy soaked up the sounds, sights, and smells of the cookcamp. He spent time outdoors, watching chipmunks and other animals and studying the workers. Inside, his grandmother bustled about the kitchen, cooking three large meals each day. At night, she sang him soft, low Norwegian lullabies. She called him "my thimble" and wrapped him in love. For Gary, the camp and the woods were magic. His grandmother was safety.

Bit by bit, Gary's grandmother learned about his life in Chicago. What Gary did not know was that his grandmother was writing fierce letters to her daughter, Eunice Paulsen, about how much Gary needed her. The letters warned Gary's mother to change her ways.

Paulsen has described his book *The Cookcamp*, based on that summer, as "almost exactly true."[2] He remembered vivid details, such as swinging his feet on a bench in a railway station and being adopted by the men of the camp.

His summer in the northern woods marked the

beginning of a lifelong romance with the wilderness—woodlands, mountains, deserts, canyons, rivers, and seas. He would use such settings again and again as powerful backdrops for the characters in his books, sometimes comparing his times in nature to a dance or a song.

That fall, Gary returned to Chicago. His mother still worked the swing shift. On weekends, worn out from her work schedule, Eunice Paulsen would nap with Gary beside her. He learned to pretend to be asleep. When she drifted off, Gary would sneak away to play.

Usually Gary stayed inside, pretending the lines in the kitchen linoleum were streets for toy cars. But one Saturday, the door was open. Clutching his toy animal, Dog, he was lured by the forbidden outside world.

The sun was bright and Gary was pulled by the color and sounds. When he needed to go to the bathroom, he relieved himself in a dark corner behind a large billboard. An old man with yellow teeth saw him. He grabbed the terrified boy and held him close to his face. Paulsen later wrote that he could smell "the stink of him," liquor and urine and vomit.[3]

Five-year-old Gary froze, unable to move or scream, knowing something bad was going to happen. Suddenly his mother was there. "Run," she screamed. Gary ran. She attacked, beating and kicking the man until he lay still.

After work or on weekends, Gary's mother sat at the kitchen table, drinking beer and reading letters from

Gary's father. Some parts she read aloud. Other parts, she said, were just for her. Then she would cry.

Lonely, Eunice Paulsen began to dress Gary in a little soldier suit and take him to bars. He sang songs she taught him or tunes from the radio. Sometimes men at the bars put coins on the counter. Gary's mother did not need the money, so she used it to buy dinner. For Gary, that part was okay.

What he did not like was when his mother stayed at the bars, drinking. Men came up to them and sat close to his mother. With her short skirts, long blond hair, and mascara, she looked to Gary like movie stars he had seen in *Life* magazine. Gary was not the only one who thought she was beautiful, and he did not like having those men around.

One day in 1945, Gary heard laughter and music and singing in the streets. World War II had ended and his father would be coming home. At last he would meet his father.

Instead, Oscar Paulsen was sent directly to the Philippines to help with the postwar rebuilding there. Gary and his mother were to sail to the Philippines to meet him. They had one week to travel across the country to San Francisco and board the ship. Quickly Eunice Paulsen packed everything they would need for two years abroad.

The airport was jammed with soldiers and sailors trying to reach the West Coast when Eunice Paulsen went to buy airline tickets. None were available, but a soldier named Matt overheard their problem. He had given up on flying and was buying a used car to drive west with another soldier. Matt asked Eunice and her son to join them. Barely hesitating, she said, "We'll go."[4]

Surrounded by luggage, the six-year-old endured a seemingly endless trip. He sat crammed into the backseat with Carl, the other soldier, who had lost his hand in the war. Gary stared at the place where the hand should have been, wondering what had happened.

Then Gary became ill. At first his mother thought he was carsick, but bright spots soon popped out on his skin. Gary's chicken pox could have kept them from boarding the ship in San Francisco, because no one with a contagious disease was allowed to leave the country. Gary was recovering, so a kind doctor agreed to skip the "diseases" box on the medical form. Then the ship's captain smuggled Gary aboard the ship at night.

A medic named Harding cared for the boy, bringing him food and reading to him in a cabin where Gary stayed all by himself. He was confined to his small white cabin for a week until his spots faded. As he began to feel better, Gary pored over *Captain Marvel*, *Superman*, and *Donald Duck* comic books.

At last Gary was free to go on deck. Everything he saw was blue—aqua water meeting blue sky. Suddenly he sensed sound, action, shouts. A frantic urgency filled the air, and Gary saw a plane, its two right propellers stalled. Realizing it was going down, he and hundreds of others ran to watch the plane circle the ship over the calm, flat sea. Sailors rushed to lower lifeboats. Harding grabbed his medic's bag and jumped into one of the boats.

The plane dropped lower and lower, and Gary felt himself lifted above the crowd to a corporal's shoulders. He watched the plane skim the surface of the water then break apart, hurling luggage, seats, and people into the water.

Women and children—military families on their way home to the United States—screamed and struggled in the wreckage. They wore life jackets, but most of them were hurt and bleeding.

Then came sharks, lured by the blood from the wounded. They attacked. It was too horrible to watch, but too horrible to look away from.

Sailors rushed to pull injured people into rescue boats. When Harding's boat returned to the ship, the bottom seemed to Gary to be awash in bright red blood.

Many of those rescued died on the deck, and the survivors had terrible wounds. Covered with blood, Gary's mother and Harding worked eighteen hours straight to help as many people as they could. Gary tried to entertain a boy named Jimmy, whose mother had died. He even gave away his beloved stuffed animal, Dog, to a little girl. The ship backtracked to Honolulu, Hawaii, where the survivors were taken ashore.

Seared into Gary Paulsen's mind forever was a picture of sharks and their helpless prey. That horrific vision of blood, bodies, and sharks still gave Gary Paulsen nightmares more than fifty years later.[5]

After that terrible incident, everyone onboard seemed to know Gary, from the engine room to the galley. He was free to roam the ship. The captain even let him hold the wheel in the pilothouse.

Their ship made one more stop before the Philippines, at the former Japanese island of Okinawa. Now that the war was over, United States soldiers were there to help rebuild the country.

At dawn, Gary watched as the ship drew into the harbor in a snowfall. The cold flakes melted as they touched the waves and the ship. Gary knew that the United States and other countries had been fighting Germany and Japan. He had a helmet and a little gun and often played war, killing pretend enemies— German and Japanese soldiers. Gary had seen real Japanese soldiers in the black-and-white images on newsreels, and he hated them.

But the Japanese people he saw now were not like that. The dock at Okinawa was filled with women and children, dressed in brightly colored silk clothing. Gary and his mother could see only four old men— most of the men had been killed in the war. The women all stood with their heads bowed. The children, begging with hands raised, were silent as the snow.

All the ideas Gary had held about Japan and its people fell away. Like him, they were children and they were hungry. "All things," Paulsen later recalled, "all my thinking, was upside down."[6]

Onshore, Gary and his mother walked through the crowd. She passed out candy and cans of condensed milk. She returned to the ship's galley for more food. When all of it was gone, one woman stepped forward. Saying nothing, she handed Eunice Paulsen her own beautiful silk kimono and fled in her simple white wrap.

The captain was furious when he learned about all the goods taken from the ship. Defiantly, Gary's mother asked, "Would you like me to catch them and take it back?"[7]

After Okinawa, the ship sailed on toward Manila in the Philippines. Gary knew they were headed toward the father he did not know.

As young as Gary Paulsen was, his mind recorded differences. His familiar world was gone. He sensed something unfamiliar about the air. Using his imagination, he called the new smell "green," like the dark green crayon in his crayon box.[8]

Three Years in the Philippines

"Everything looked blown to pieces."[1]

Sailing into the port city of Manila in the Philippines, Gary saw the ruins of war—rubble, cratered roads, ruined buildings.

The father he had imagined for so long was not at the dock. Colonel Oscar Paulsen had sent an aide, Sergeant Ryland, for Gary and Eunice Paulsen.

As they drove through the entry gate of their housing compound, six-year-old Gary saw soldiers with machine guns. Sergeant Ryland explained that the guns were because of guerrilla fighters. Gary misunderstood. He did not know that *guerrillas* meant local underground fighters. To him, the word sounded like "gorillas." He pictured huge, hairy apes storming the base.

The gate marked the change from dirty to orderly. The Paulsens' house was built on three-foot stilts,

The Paulsens' house in the Philippines was raised on stilts and had screens for walls because the climate was so hot.

and lizards roamed the walls inside. Because the climate was hot, walls of the house were just screens. Filipino servants, Rom and Maria, had been hired to help Eunice Paulsen.

Then Gary's father arrived, no longer a man in a small black-and-white photo, but tall and real. Shy at first, Gary was coaxed to hug this father he had never known. He started to tell his father about their trip. "There'll be time for all of it later—we've got all the time in the world now," Oscar Paulsen told his son. Later, Gary Paulsen wrote, "Because I was young and didn't know any better I believed him."[2]

For a while, Gary and his mother did everything together. Soon, though, she slipped into her role as an officer's wife. Gary explored the whole compound alone. One day he climbed inside a badly rusted tank to play soldier. Rom scrubbed all the rust off Gary and his clothes before his mother found out.

In 1946, on the one vacation the family took while in the Philippines, Gary got his first dog. He pleaded for a small black hound that was about to be killed for food. His mother bargained with a Filipino man to buy it. Because of the white circle on the lean puppy's side, Gary named him Snowball. For Gary's three years in the Philippines, the boy and his short-haired dog went everywhere together.

Gary could see the signs of war—overturned Jeeps, wrecked houses, rusting guns, shell casings— "but Snowball would *know* things," wrote Paulsen later. "She would see the obvious outside way a thing looked, but then she would move to it and smell it and perhaps lick it and dig at it and look under it, and I took to doing the same things."[3]

Snowball even saved the seven-year-old's life. One day, Gary was stepping toward what looked like a pretty ribbon on a trail when the ribbon—a deadly snake—moved. Snowball flew past Gary and killed the snake.

Gary had many experiences in the Philippines that would have been shocking even for adults. On a visit to Sandiago Prison, he saw where a friend of his father had died after being tortured. During a terrible typhoon, Gary saw a man killed by a sheet of flying metal. He watched Rom kill a twelve-foot snake that had swallowed the next-door neighbors' monkey. With Rom, Gary explored a cave filled with bones and decomposing bodies where many Japanese soldiers had died.

As time passed, Eunice Paulsen laughed less and played less with Gary. He could smell beer and gin on his parents' breath. They paid little attention to him. Gary was on his own.

One evening, Sergeant Ryland drove the Paulsens to a fancy party at a mansion. Dressed up in a too-tight suit, Gary was to meet the new mayor of Manila. After the dinner, Gary was sent outside to play with some Filipino children who were taking turns jumping from a high stone stairway.

Ryland taunted him to go all the way to the top. Gary did. Then he jumped, landing so hard that he bit his tongue almost completely off. Only sinew, a ribbon of tissue, held it. Blood gushed. Ryland and Gary's mother raced him to the base hospital. Without giving him any painkillers, doctors matter-of-factly went to work. Gary felt every one of the eleven stitches taken in his tongue.

Another time, when Colonel Paulsen and Sergeant Ryland had to go to another island on business, Gary and his mother went along. Once on the island, they rode in dugout canoes and stopped for lunch by a stream. As Gary waded in, he went under, helplessly caught in a swift current. A Filipino boy dived in and saved Gary from drowning. As soon as her son was safe, Eunice Paulsen forced him back into the water so he would not be afraid of it later on.

The boy was more and more alone. In the daytime, Gary's father was busy with his work. His mother was at the Officers' Club, or playing cards and gossiping with other officers' wives. Nighttime brought more drinking, then fights. His parents had no idea what their young son was doing, thinking, or discovering. He had a secret life of his own.

One day Gary saw Rom take two cans of sardines from a shelf. If Gary reported the stealing, Rom would never be able to get another job and his family would starve. After that, Rom did anything Gary wanted. Gary told Rom to take him "outside," beyond the wire of the military housing compound.

With a bicycle for transportation, Gary explored other parts of the island. No matter where they went, he always felt safe with Rom. Gary even grew to like "baloots," which he later described as ducks killed inside their eggs just before hatching, the eggs then buried in the sand. He and Rom swallowed baloots in

Far from his Midwest upbringing, young Gary found himself in a world of lizards, palm trees, soldiers, and wartime devastation in the Philippines.

a single gulp, and, said Paulsen, "they were especially good chased with warm Coca-Cola."[4]

In the Philippines, Gary's schooling was spotty, as it would be all his life. He had no friends his own age. His home life was empty, and relations between his parents were growing steadily worse.

For Gary, his dog Snowball became almost like a parent, watching out for the lonely boy.[5] When it was time to go back to the United States, Gary refused to go without Snowball. His parents tackled the pile of paperwork required for taking a dog from the Philippines to the United States.

Two weeks before they were to leave, Gary and Snowball were walking down the road when a truck carrying Filipino soldiers swerved. It deliberately hit Snowball, and she died instantly. Gary stood, "not believing she was dead, thinking how nothing would ever be right again, not ever, and how I would always, always miss her, and that is all true," Paulsen later wrote.[6]

Soon after, Eunice Paulsen fell apart. Her emotional breakdown was made worse by her drinking. Six days after Christmas in 1949, ten-year-old Gary and his mother flew back to the United States.

Despite her neglect, much of Gary Paulsen's sense of what was right and wrong came from his mother. His mother hated injustice, and she hated the horrors of war. The boy knew when his mother was angry or upset about something because "her back got all stiff and her voice sounded flat."[7] If action was needed, she took it quickly. From finding food for the

Japanese in Okinawa to demanding higher pay for Maria and Rom, she did what she thought was right.

Paulsen's own sense of the stupidity and uselessness of war was formed in the Philippines. He remembered Sergeant Ryland's words: "No part of war—no part is building. It's all tearing apart."[8]

For young Gary, worse experiences were to come.

The Runaway Years

"My life was a horror."[1]

Colonel Paulsen returned to the United States and was stationed at the Pentagon, the main military headquarters, for his last nine months of duty. The family lived in Washington, D.C. After he left the Army, the Paulsens returned to northern Minnesota. Oscar Paulsen started a chicken farm forty miles north of Laporte, Minnesota; then they moved west to Thief River Falls.

With Gary's parents drinking more heavily than ever, he found safety living with relatives. As an adult, Paulsen joked that "everybody north of Bemidji is related to me."[2] Many times, he worked and lived on his uncles' farms to get away from home. This gave Gary the stability so lacking in his own home.

Later, Paulsen used humor to capture his summer

adventures with a cousin on a farm in the comical *Harris and Me: A Summer Remembered.* "We'd get up, have breakfast and get in trouble. That's all we did," said Paulsen.[3] The zany stories overlay a young boy's poignant memories of parents whose lives were ruled by beer and whiskey. With his uncles and aunts, he felt at last that he belonged and was loved. Farm memories were also central to Paulsen's book *Popcorn Days and Buttermilk Nights.*

Gary's relatives were like anchors in his stormy life. Strong and steady, his hardworking uncles knew farming. They showed him what it was to work from

This Minnesota farm is typical of the ones where Gary Paulsen spent his summers, living with uncles, aunts, and cousins.

dawn to dark, plowing fields, harvesting, feeding animals. His uncles were born storytellers, too.

The gentleness of his grandmother and aunts was also important to Gary. He learned as he watched them at their chores and saw how families could work. He observed their mending, cooking, baking, and gardening. Grandmother Alida even taught him to crochet. The women in his life showed Gary a feminine side. From them, he learned compassion.

Despite the kindness of relatives, Gary Paulsen endured long, hard years while growing up. He has described his childhood as "ugly."[4] His parents had become the town drunks, drinking and fighting, fighting and drinking. In most ways, his childhood was a nightmare.

Gary was terribly shy. With his lack of social skills and his family troubles, he led a solitary life. He found ways to escape from the fights and drinking at home. Most of those ways meant being alone.

When Gary was twelve years old, he had an idea. If he could touch a deer, maybe he would be more popular with his classmates. He knew that deer can sprint to escape predators, but they cannot run long distances without resting. Relentlessly, he tracked a doe—a female deer—for two days, until she was completely out of wind. At last, he moved in close and touched the exhausted, terrified animal.

When he reported this at school, however, it did nothing to increase his popularity. No one believed him. Still, he had learned. He held the deer and his knowledge of her in his memory. Years later, touching a deer became the core of his book *Tracker*.

That same year, an uncle gave him a Remington .22 rifle for hunting. Gary hunted ruffed grouse, rabbits, and other small game. He carried bread, matches, and a small pot with him so he could cook the meat and make a meal.

Gary longed for a friend. He found one unexpectedly when he sneaked from the family's apartment in Twin Forks to go hunting in the early morning. Something growled in the darkness. Was it a bear?

He was ready to shoot, forgetting his gun was not loaded, when he realized that it was a big black dog, a Labrador retriever. His tag read, "My name is Ike." Gary soon discovered that Ike knew hunting.

After that, Gary and the dog met every morning. Ike retrieved the ducks Gary shot during hunting season. Gary told the dog all his troubles, with Ike's "huge brown eyes looking up at me while I petted him and rattled on," said Paulsen.[5]

One day Ike did not show up to meet Gary. Although the dog never came back, he had been a friend when Gary had needed one most. Paulsen learned years later that Ike never hunted again. The faithful dog stayed loyally by the side of his former master after he returned in a wheelchair from the Korean War.

Gary's school life in Minnesota was as random as it had been in the Philippines. Whenever the Paulsens moved, it meant a new school for Gary. A new school meant patchy learning and fights. He played hooky more often than not and did poorly in classes when he did attend. He was chosen last for sports and thought of himself as an idiot.[6]

As a teenager, "I was . . . a geek, a nerd, a dweeb," Paulsen said.[7] Gary missed most of ninth grade, flunked it, and had to repeat.

To avoid his parents and the apartment, Gary used the basement of their grubby tenement building as a hideaway. By the furnace, an old armchair with sticking-out springs became his refuge. He would take peanut butter, Ritz crackers, and a quart of milk to the basement, where he daydreamed, made model airplanes, and read comics by a light that hung from the ceiling.[8]

Often Gary spent the night in the basement, too, away from his parents' constant arguments and negligence. Despite being sure that nothing good was ever going to happen to him, he was learning to fend for himself.[9]

Gary began spending nights, even weekends, in the woods. Sometimes he skipped whole weeks of school at a time. He lived in a small town, with no counselors or agencies to help a child in trouble. "I ran to the woods and rivers of northern Minnesota . . . a kind of self-fostering. . . ," Paulsen later wrote. "In the woods or fishing on the rivers and lakes our lives didn't hurt."[10]

Gary grew to love the outdoors—the times fishing with other boys, the times of solitude—developing a bond with living things and nature. His teenage years spent in the North Woods would make the rest of his life bend toward a reverence for nature. They also raised in him questions about the right to take the life of another living creature. Years later, he would write about these times in *Father Water, Mother Woods: Essays on Fishing and Hunting in the North Woods.*

A momentous event, one that would color the rest of his days, took place one freezing winter night when Gary was fourteen. All Gary wanted was shelter from the cold, and he stepped into a building to get warm. It was a library, a place he had never been. The librarian asked him if he wanted a book. "I said 'Sure,' kind of cocky," Paulsen wrote later.[11]

The librarian handed him a western. Back home, as Gary struggled to read the book, he was constantly forced to backtrack, reading some parts over and over. Word by word, he struggled to make sense of the story. It took him a month to read that one book.

Although Paulsen does not remember the librarian's name, the day she gave him a library card with his name on it marked a turning point in his life. She always had books waiting for him when he returned the ones he had read. Gradually his reading skills improved, and by summer he was roaring through a book a day. The librarian guided his choices, slipping books like Herman Melville's *Moby Dick* in with westerns and adventure books.

"It was as though I had been dying of thirst and the librarian had handed me a five-gallon bucket of water. I drank and drank," he said.[12] "The only reason I'm here and not in prison is because of that woman. I was a loser, but she showed me the power of reading, that I didn't need to qualify with the right clothes. Everything I am I owe to that woman."[13]

By then, life with his parents was so destructive that the fourteen-year-old regularly left home. At first,

As a teenager, Gary Paulsen had a miserable family life and no close friends.

he took to the streets. Later he ran away. Gary lived by his wits, teetering on the edge of serious trouble.

The young teen took whatever work he could find. He sold newspapers and set pins in bowling alleys. Before automatic pinsetters, bowling pins had to be reset by hand each time they toppled. The pinsetter could be hit by a stray bowling ball. It was dangerous, mind-numbing work. Although the job gave him money for clothes, they were never the right kind and it was never enough money.

Late at night when the bowling alley closed, Gary would head for home. This put him on the streets at the same time as a roving gang of boys with switch-blade knives. Those bullies were out for trouble.

"I became their favorite target in this dark world," said Paulsen.[14] One night, trying a new route back to the apartment, he left the bowling alley by the roof. When he clambered down the outside of the building, he stepped down on a growling dog.

To escape, Gary tossed the dog half a hamburger, his only dinner. Gary ran from the dog right into the gang. As the boys began to beat him, he heard snarls, then yelling. He saw a "big, tough, mean alley dog. As I watched he spit cloth—it looked like blue jeans—out of his mouth."[15] When the gang fled, Gary fed the dog the rest of the hamburger and named him "Dirk" after a tough guy in a book he was reading.

"Dirk was like a pet alligator," said Paulsen.[16]

The next time the gang went after Gary, Dirk bit the leader in the stomach. From then on, Dirk was in on all Gary's fights. "I'd kinda aim him" in their direction, said Paulsen.[17] At last Gary was free of the gang's cruelty. Even after Dirk later found a new life with a farmer named Olaf, the gang left Gary alone.

One icy winter night, Gary was about to steal a pair of skis from a garage to sell for money. A hard-nosed policeman, called J.D., caught him. He put Gary in the back of the patrol car. Gary assumed he was going to jail, but instead J.D. drove a long distance out of town.

When he told Gary to get out of the car and walk, Gary protested. The temperature was twenty degrees below zero. "If you keep moving, you won't die," the policeman responded.[18] In the squad car's headlights, Gary plodded seven miles back into town, his hands clamped over his ears to keep them from freezing.

At the edge of town, J.D. asked if he ever planned to steal again. "No," said Gary.[19] Then J.D. asked Gary if he was hungry. Even though he was often hungry, Gary did not answer. "That's what I thought," said J.D.[20] He drove Gary to Harry's Diner, an all-night café. Gary wolfed down meatloaf, potatoes, green beans, milk, and a big chunk of stale apple pie.

J.D.'s hard exterior masked his concern for Gary, especially the night they saw Gary's drunken father staggering home down an alley. For two years, Gary met J.D. at Harry's after a night of setting pins. J.D. became a substitute father, teaching Gary lessons in life and nurturing him through the bad times.

In the summer of 1955, sixteen-year-old Gary ran away to North Dakota to hoe the beet fields with Mexican migrant workers. They adopted this smallish boy trying to make it on his own, fed him, and talked to him as a human being, not the son of drunks. The backbreaking work he did honed in him a deep admiration for the workers. This experience shaped his strong sense of what was fair and unfair.

Later, as a writer, Paulsen based *Tiltawhirl John* on his adventures as a runaway working in beet fields and at a carnival. From the book, readers sense the terrible monotony of hoeing beets with a sawed-off hoe—step and cut, step and cut, the endless rows of beets, the calluses and aching back. In *Sentries*, too, when David hoes beets, readers know that nothing about the work is invented. Gary Paulsen lived it.

The next summer, Gary found a job in Waseca, a town near Minnesota's southern border, four hundred miles from his home. He packed boxes of Birdseye frozen foods, earning $1.05 an hour, a huge sum to him. With no place to live in Waseca, he moved in with a childhood friend in Mankato, almost thirty miles from the factory.

Paulsen slept on a couch, rising at four each morning to walk or hitchhike to work. Often, he was late. A foreman gave Gary a used bicycle with a small motor, called a Whizzer, so he could get to work more easily. By pedaling hard until the motor caught, he could speed along at twenty miles an hour. Away from home, Gary had freedom, transportation, and a job. It was a marvelous summer.

Gary Paulsen has said of his childhood, "I had a rough run."[21] He had no support from his alcoholic parents, no social life, and terrible grades in school. Because of this, Gary learned to rely on himself as he grew up. He earned money, bought clothing, hunted for food. Perhaps most important, he taught himself to read. Books were a miracle in his life, opening a larger world to him.

The steadiness of relatives, a caring librarian, and J.D., the small-town policeman, helped Gary get through his deeply troubled teen years. Despite his unstable home life, he attended school long enough to squeak by with grades in the D-minus range, graduating from Lincoln High School in Thief River Falls in 1957. He took pre-engineering classes at Bemidji State Teachers College in 1957 and 1958, earning money by trapping destructive animals for the state of Minnesota. Once again, his grades slipped, and he flunked out of college.

Then, in a surprise decision, he followed in his father's footsteps.

5

Bad Times

"I thought 'I'm on my way. . . .' And I just destroyed myself."[1]

Early in 1959, Gary Paulsen forged his parents' signatures and joined the Army. He was nineteen, and he saw the Army as a way out of a hard life. "I knew four hours in that I'd made a mistake," he said later.[2] Paulsen can still tell anyone exactly how many days and minutes he spent in the service, but the Army served him well.

During basic training at Fort Carson, Colorado, a stern drill sergeant saw something in the tough, surly teen. "It took that sergeant about three days to straighten me out," said Paulsen. "I'd fought all my life but I couldn't beat him."[3] The sergeant helped Gary realize that he had to get his life squared away.

They became friends after that, and Gary worked hard, entering the Army missile training program.

Stationed at a missile school at Fort Bliss, Texas, Paulsen took engineering and technology courses. He rose to the rank of sergeant. Sometimes when they were off duty, Paulsen and a friend crossed the near-by border into Mexico to try to help the young children who lived on the streets of Juárez. He would later draw on his Army days to write *The Crossing* and *Canyons*.

Nineteen and immature, Paulsen got married. He later called it a "young come-home-on-leave-from-the Army marriage, the learn-how-little-you-know-about-other-people marriage."[4] Soon the couple had a child.

A year later, a friend wrote Paulsen with bad news. Officer J.D. was dead. A runaway boy had shot J.D. as he tried to persuade the boy to return home. Paulsen was devastated. He thought about getting even by going after J.D.'s killer, but avenging J.D.'s death could land him in prison. Since he now had a wife and a child, Paulsen could not afford the risk.

When Paulsen left the Army in May 1962, he went into electronics. Five years earlier, in 1957, Russia had launched *Sputnik I*, the first satellite to orbit the earth. The United States was racing to catch up. Paulsen used his Army training and other courses to become a certified field engineer. For three years, he tracked satellites in California for aerospace companies.

By then he had two children, but his marriage was falling apart. When he was just twenty-six years old, and in the process of getting a divorce, Paulsen's life took an abrupt turn. Sitting at work, tracking a *Mariner* space probe, he made a snap decision to become a writer. Reading an article in a magazine about flight testing, Paulsen suddenly decided that writing would be a good way to make a living. All he would have to do, Paulsen thought, was to first find work editing magazines. He turned off the console in front of him, handed his top-security badge to a startled guard, and left the job, never to return.

Gary Paulsen had no basis for this instant decision to become a writer. Writing was not a lifelong dream. He had received consistently bad grades, taken no writing courses, and not finished college. All of a sudden, writing was just something he knew he had to do. He had an instantaneous, urgent need to write.

Paulsen headed for Hollywood. With a résumé he created for himself ("my first piece of fiction," said Paulsen), he became an associate editor at a men's magazine.[5] His employer soon realized that Paulsen had no editing experience. Seeing how serious he was about learning to write, three editors became his teachers.

Paulsen learned on the job. During the day, he worked at the magazine, and at night he worked on assignments the editors gave him. The next day they reviewed his work. Inch by inch, Paulsen's writing skills and confidence grew.

While in Hollywood, Paulsen married again. He also worked as a movie extra—hired for minor parts—and did wood carving. A piece of his sculpture came close to winning first prize in an exhibition. His creativity pulled him two ways, but Paulsen realized that he could not be both an artist and a writer. Writing won.

Wisely, Paulsen began to see that he had "started to get pulled into Hollywood. It's so seductive, the money and the beautiful people. I left fast . . . I was terrified that I would become a Hollywood writer."[6]

Ending his short-lived second marriage, Paulsen quit his job and fled Hollywood for the place he knew as home. He drove a Volkswagen Beetle from California all the way to Laporte in northern Minnesota. His needs were few and Paulsen knew the woods, so he could survive without money.

His first work, *The Special War*, published in 1966, was written with coauthor Raymond Friday Locke. It was based on a series of interviews with Vietnam War veterans.

Paulsen spent the winter in a cabin rented for $25 a month. For food, Paulsen caught fish, spearing them through holes in the ice. He ate deer meat and rabbit, which is hard to clean. "I got sick of spitting rabbit fur," he said.[7]

By the time spring came, twenty-seven-year-old Gary Paulsen had sold his first book manuscript. In the nonfictional *Some Birds Don't Fly*, he mixed humor with satire to give his views of the missile industry. *Mr. Tucket*, his first fictional book for young readers, sold soon after.

Buoyed by these sales, he briefly moved back to California. Then, late in 1967, he moved to Taos, New Mexico. With two book sales, he thought that he could

This Minnesota map shows Clearwater Lake as well as some of the small towns where Gary Paulsen has lived. (The Twin Cities— Minneapolis and the state capital, St. Paul—are shown for reference.)

fit in with the many artists and writers who lived there.

Instead his life spiraled downward. The problems of growing up with alcoholic parents caught up with him at last. He began to drink in 1967 and kept at it for six straight years.

Paulsen was twenty-eight when his first two books were published in 1968. As his drinking grew worse, writing became harder and harder for him. His first wife remarried and his two children were adopted by her new husband.

One morning in 1969, Paulsen stood in line at a Taos post office. He had no way of knowing how important that day would be for him. Two people he knew to be FBI agents walked in. The FBI had been wondering if he had given away government secrets about missiles in *Some Birds Don't Fly*. He still does not know why the book had drawn attention from the FBI; he just hoped the agents were not looking for him.[8]

Paulsen had $20 with him, his pay for a magazine story he had written. He did not want to lose it, so for safekeeping he handed his wallet to the woman behind him in line. That is how he met Ruth Ellen Wright, a teacher and artist. "When I looked into those eyes, I fell in love. I knew this was the woman I'd marry," said Paulsen.[9]

Nothing came of the FBI investigation, but Ruth Wright and Gary Paulsen started seeing each other. They moved together in 1969 from Taos to Colorado and were married in 1971 in Denver. Their son,

James Wright Paulsen, was born at the end of the year.

Living with his wife and baby in a little cottage, Paulsen worked as a laborer during the day and tried to write at night. The family had a huge Great Dane named Caesar. Paulsen would later write a hilarious chapter about Caesar's escapades in *My Life in Dog Years*.

But Paulsen, four years into a time of heavy drinking, was just drifting from job to job. He worked with hot roofing tar and gravel, cut trees in a ski area in four feet of snow, hauled bricks up scaffolding, drove heavy trucks, did demolition, and built houses.

His worst job, one he called "odious," was with a septic tank company that replaced old tanks with new ones. As the newest employee, he was the one to empty sewage—human waste—from the old tanks. Sometimes homeowners accidentally flushed their toilets while Paulsen was shoveling. The other workers thought it was a great joke when the waste then spewed down on him.

The drinking days were a dark time for Gary Paulsen. He brawled in bars, picked fights, and lost every one. He could not keep a job or write. He despaired, often threatening to end his life. Through it all, Ruth Paulsen "was a tremendously positive and insistent force" in his survival, his editor Richard Jackson said later.[10]

After years of alcohol abuse, Paulsen's family life was falling apart. One terrible morning in 1973, Gary Paulsen reached bottom. He passed out at a friend's house in Taos, almost four hundred miles from his

Colorado home. He came to with his two-year-old son next to him.

In that awful moment, Paulsen knew that he was repeating all his parents' mistakes. He was thirty-four and had lost six years to alcohol. Not only was he ruining his own life, he was ruining Ruth's and Jim's, too.

He vowed to stop drinking.

After trying to quit on his own, he sought help. On May 5, 1973, the second anniversary of his marriage to Ruth, Gary Paulsen stopped drinking for good. He made it through the first rocky days without a drink and stayed both sober and happily married after that.

The heavy drinking, though, had taken its toll. Paulsen struggled for two years to find his writing voice once again. It was so difficult that he almost gave up in 1975.

At last, the books started coming. Paulsen wrote for adults, both fiction and nonfiction books based on his construction work. He also coauthored a young adult biography of Martin Luther King, Jr., with writer Dan Theis. Then Paulsen, who admitted he was terrible at sports, wrote a series of sports books with goofy titles, such as *Dribbling, Shooting, and Scoring—Sometimes* and *Running, Jumping, and Throwing—If You Can.*

In 1976, his young adult novel *Winterkill* was published, followed the next year by *Tiltawhirl John. The Foxman* and *The Night the White Deer Died* came out in 1978. Once, a friend made a bet with him to see how fast he could work. Paulsen wrote eleven articles and stories in just four days and sold every one.

Gary Paulsen's life was changing dramatically. Jim was starting school and Ruth was working on her art. Gary's drinking problems were behind him. He had written close to two hundred stories and articles for magazines and more than thirty books.

Just as he was gaining confidence in his work, more trouble came. He signed a contract with a new publisher and borrowed money against the contract. The books were published, but Paulsen was not paid. It was a disaster. The Paulsens went deeply into debt. They left Colorado and retreated to the familiar woods of northern Minnesota late in 1979.

Then came another blow. Paulsen was sued for libel, for supposedly damaging someone's reputation. Some people felt that characters in one of his books were too close to people Gary Paulsen had actually known.

"The whole situation was so nasty and ugly that I stopped writing. I wanted nothing more to do with publishing and burned my bridges, so to speak," he said. He now calls it "all a misunderstanding," but it was a very grim time. The case was dismissed by both a lower court and the Minnesota State Supreme Court, "but it brought me to the edge of bankruptcy," he said.[11]

Once again, Gary Paulsen had hit rock bottom.

Then Storm, Yogi, Obeah, and Columbia came into his life.

Paulsen's Life as a Dog

"I had learned that I knew absolutely nothing."[1]

Back in Minnesota, Gary Paulsen and his wife were so poor that they "lived under flat rocks and ate bugs," he would later tease.[2] Their home was little more than a shack, with no indoor plumbing or electricity. To get to school, their son, Jim, rode five hours round-trip on a bus each day.

"We made our own ketchup. We made everything. We had goats. We made butter and cheese," said Paulsen.[3] Three large vegetable gardens provided much of their food. They ate beaver meat and other game to survive.

Paulsen could not stop writing, and he knew he had to learn more. He began traveling, speaking, teaching writing, and listening to other writers at workshops and conventions.

While Paulsen's artist wife painted, he turned to the tedious job of trapping beavers and coyotes. He did this for food and to earn bounty money—pay from the government of Minnesota for controlling the destructive animals. Early each morning, he started out on foot or on skis to check his twenty-mile trapline, returning late each night. For this, Paulsen earned $2,000 a year.

Hearing about Paulsen's struggles, a man provided transportation—a broken sled and four older dogs: Storm, Yogi, Obeah, and Columbia. Trained for twelve-mile sprints, they could get untangled and line up on their own. But there was one problem: Not one of the four was a leader. They just sat there. For two weeks Paulsen hitched himself to the sled and became the lead dog, teaching them. Eventually, Storm took the lead.

The Paulsens had no car. The dogs pulled the Paulsens to the Laundromat in town and hauled wood. With the team, Paulsen could now cover sixty to eighty miles of traplines in three days' time.

Then a new dog came into his life. Cookie was hungry, ill, and lame—so thin her ribs stuck out. In two days, Cookie ate a whole seventy-five-pound beaver carcass. After medical treatment for worms, she recovered well. Hitched to the team, she kept jumping up, looking over the dog ahead of her to see what was happening. Dog by dog, Paulsen moved her up. With Cookie as leader, Paulsen began making three-day runs, camping at night.

The next year, Paulsen's income rose to $3,000. Although he knew little more about running dogs

than "Gee" for right and "Haw" for left, he learned
from his team.

The lessons came fast.

Several times he stubbornly ordered a team to go
to the right or go to the left. After many accidents and
near-accidents, he understood at last that he could—
and should—trust his dogs.

In January of 1980, Paulsen was working a spot
on a seventy-five-mile trapline. His dog team napped
nearby. During winter, danger lurks on lakes where
beavers build their lodges. Ice stays thin near lodges,
even with temperatures at fifty degrees below zero.
Trapped air bubbles and the beavers' backs brushing
the surface of the ice below the water keep the ice
from getting thick.

Paulsen took a step onto some fragile ice. In a
flash he was in dire trouble.

Instinctively, he grabbed the rope that tied the
supplies to his sled. Plunging downward into the
frigid water, he let out a terrified yelp. Cookie woke
and their eyes locked.

The next second he was twelve feet under, in icy
water. "You go down like a stone. It's so fast, you don't
float at all," said Paulsen.[4]

Frigid water kills quickly, and the memory of several friends who had died that way zinged into
Paulsen's mind. "All these bubbles are my life and
there it goes," he thought.[5]

Paulsen tried to reach the surface, but his clothes
were too heavy. He could not move from the bottom of
the lake. Suddenly the line in his hands went taut.
Cookie had roused the rest of the team. They pulled

and pulled, hauling Paulsen from the water and onto stronger ice.

Stunned, he knew he had only seconds to act before his clothes froze. Quaking with cold, with the temperature thirty degrees below zero, he tossed cooking kerosene on a pine tree and lit a huge fire for warmth. The heat kept his zippers from freezing shut, and he was able to shuck off his sopping clothes and fumble into a sleeping bag. "And all the while I'm hugging this dog," he said.[6]

For Cookie, the whole incident was business— "The dummy fell through the ice. We saved the dummy," said Paulsen, imagining Cookie's thoughts.[7]

On another run, twenty miles from home, he flew from the sled, ripping open his kneecap. He passed out from the pain. Dog teams usually keep running even if the musher falls off, so Paulsen was in serious trouble. Luck was with him that day. Obeah, the lead dog, somehow turned the dogs around and scrabbled down a steep bank, dragging behind him a tangle of dogs and the sled. Another dog, Duberry, offered first aid, gently licking Paulsen's wound clean. Dazed, Paulsen crawled onto the sled and the team pulled him home. From this, he came to understand that the dogs "had great, old knowledge," as he later wrote in *Woodsong*.[8]

Paulsen began to rethink his ideas about animals. As he had done as a child with his first dog, Snowball, he now became a student, observing how his dogs and other animals behaved. He listened to an old cowhand tell how cows out on the range baby-sat for one another. The cows would take turns watching over the

Paulsen says that his lead dog Cookie, above, saved his life—
"three times that I know of, maybe more that I wasn't aware of."

young calves while one cow walked a long distance for water, too far for the calves to walk.

A final lesson came when Columbia played a trick on another dog. Because sled dogs tend to fight, Paulsen's dogs were each chained near their own huts in the kennel. Sometimes the Paulsens gave out chewing bones so the dogs would not be bored. Columbia's hut was next to Olaf's. Olaf was aggressive, and not too bright. Columbia had always steered clear of him.

One day Paulsen saw that Columbia had left tasty bits of meat on his chewing bone. Columbia inched the bone to a spot just beyond Olaf's reach. The tip of

Olaf's claw could barely touch the bone, and the dog went crazy trying to reach it.

"Columbia had measured it to the millimeter," said Paulsen. "Columbia leaned back and laughed. 'Heh, heh, heh . . . ,'" said Paulsen.[9] The dog had played a trick and been amused when it worked. If a dog could do that, then other animals could, too.

Gary Paulsen had hunted all his life, but now his observations about animals interfered. When he saw that they could plan and think, he abruptly realized that he could no longer trap and kill animals. The lesson of animal intelligence was so strong that both Ruth and Gary Paulsen became vegetarians, never again eating meat.

In kennels, sled dogs often sleep in individual wooden huts, like these. They are kept separate so they cannot fight.

The Paulsens continued to live very simply in their small, wood-sided home. Wonderful smells filled the air—garlic, dried fish, and foods from the gardens. Stew often bubbled on the woodstove used for both cooking and heating.

At their home on the edge of the wilderness, the family kept other animals besides dogs—chickens, geese, ducks, cats. The scent of their feed drew skunks, foxes, coyotes, ravens, weasels, bears, even an eagle.

Despite their uneasy truce with bears, both Gary and Ruth Paulsen had close calls. One persistent bear swiped off the side of the enclosure used for trash burning. Angered, Paulsen threw a stick at him. "I have made many mistakes in my life . . . but I hope never to throw a stick at a bear again," remembered Paulsen.[10] Rising onto its hind legs, the bear towered over him.

Paulsen froze, helpless. He could not move, could not think. Something made the bear back down and lumber off. In that heart-stopping moment, Paulsen learned another profound lesson. To the bear, he was just another animal, nothing special because of being human.

Another problem bear kept returning despite warning shots fired over his head. Gary Paulsen was not home the day that bear moved toward Ruth as she weeded the garden. She did all the right things, backing up slowly and not making eye contact. It did not work. The bear prepared to attack.

He did not count on Quincy, a tiny, unpredictable mutt that looked, said Paulsen, like "a dust mop that had been dropped in grease and rolled in old coffee grounds."[11] Quincy was not about to let a bear threaten Ruth.

The scraggly dog leapt for the huge bear, grabbed its chest, and held on. "My wife chose that moment to use all the good luck from the rest of her life," said Paulsen.[12] Instead of fleeing, she ran toward the bear. She plucked Quincy away, and raced with him for the house. Whether confused or startled, the bear gave up the attack.

Then came the magical run with his dogs on Clearwater Lake and beyond that transformed Paulsen. After his team seemed to become a steam ghost in the moonlight, he drove on, over other frozen lakes, through trees, in and out of Canada. *Dogteam*, his 1993 picture book, captures the mystical wonder of a nighttime dogsledding run. With his rhythmic words, even the dogs sing their joy. Ruth Paulsen created the vibrant illustrations in the book.

Paulsen kept running his dogs. Skimming over frozen lakes and scudding on trails glistening with snow, he and the dogs ran for the joy of it. The beauty of the North Woods called to him, and he was filled with wonder at the dogs themselves.

In Minnesota, though, dog teams were work teams. Paulsen knew that running dogs without trapping would look odd. For cover, he went through the motions of checking traplines as he ran his team. He even changed territory as good trappers do. He just set no traps.

Paulsen's sled runs sometimes lasted several nights and covered several hundred miles. Now, a single word

Artist Ruth Wright Paulsen painted this picture of her husband, Gary, working with his sled dogs.

gave him a reason for running dogs that had nothing to do with trapping: Iditarod!

The Iditarod, a 1,049-mile dogsled race across Alaska, commemorates a lifesaving dogsled run made in 1925 to get medication for diphtheria to Nome from north of Anchorage. Running the Iditarod was like mushing all the way from Los Angeles, California, to Seattle, Washington, with higher mountains, rougher terrain, freezing weather, and howling winds.

Gary Paulsen made a decision: He would run in the 1983 Iditarod. To get ready, the Paulsens began buying and trading more and more dogs. In a time they called "The Great Kennel Invasion," the Paulsens' dogs were having pups.[13] They had also bought four other litters of puppies.

One spring morning Paulsen woke to find thirty-six puppies waiting to get into the house. To his credit, he did hesitate. Then he opened the door. The puppies tumbled in, licking, sniffing, exploring. They swarmed over his wife and son, rousting them from their beds. The pups were headed for the pantry before he could get them all back outside.

As the dogs grew, Paulsen began to train them year-round. The dogs' eagerness, combined with his lack of knowledge, made for many wild rides. In winter, the teams pulled sleds. In warmer weather, with no snow, he used a wheeled sled. Once Paulsen tried a bicycle behind the team, but it proved far too light. He bought a stripped-down car that the dogs pulled easily.

In winter and in summer, he had wrecks he could not believe he lived through. Sometimes the dogs took a sharp turn, but the sled did not make it and skidded sideways. Sometimes a rabbit crossed their path and the dogs took off on surprise side trips through the woods. Sometimes Paulsen lost the dogs completely and had to walk miles home through swarms of mosquitoes and mucky bogs.

On one run, he started out with wooden matches in his pockets. When he lost his grip and dragged along the ground, the matches lit and his pants caught fire. "My wife said I left the yard like a meteorite!" he remembered.[14]

Paulsen put everything he could into the training. He moved in with the dogs, sewing, reading, and sleeping in the kennel. Often Paulsen sang along as the dogs' songs filled the nighttime air, and later he wrote about the "round sound that is so eerie and hauntingly beautiful."[15]

He gave the dogs training, food, booties, shoulder rubs, and love. "What they give you is *everything*," said Paulsen.[16]

It took money to enter and run the Iditarod. Paulsen would need $14,000—for him, a huge sum. His hometown of Bemidji rallied behind him, with potluck suppers, raffles, dances, sponsorships, even an old truck.

An important phone call came when the Iditarod fund-raising was getting down to the wire. Despite the heavy training schedule, Paulsen was still writing. His article "The Deer" appeared in *U.S. Catholic*, and book editor Richard Jackson, of Bradbury Press, liked what he read. He asked Paulsen to write for him, but Paulsen said he was too busy training. "I'll send you the money," replied Jackson, "and when you get around to writing something, let me be the first to see it."[17]

A man who donated an old Chevy pickup took time off to drive with Paulsen to Alaska. He volunteered to keep the truck going and help handle the dogs during training. They set off, pulling a trailer with twenty dogs, driving in temperatures often colder than fifty degrees below zero.

Just getting to Alaska was an adventure, as Paulsen hauled the dogs in terrible weather over thousands of miles of bad roads. Ruth and young Jim joined Paulsen after he arrived and helped gather supplies and continue training. The mountains of Alaska made Minnesota seem flat. The dogs balked at the first steep incline they came to.

Gary Paulsen's approach to the Iditarod was different from other mushers'. His idea was not winning but having a great adventure. To him, it was a long, long run, not a race, and he loved running. He wanted to be with the beauty, to test himself, and to be one with his dogs. In the Iditarod, he said, "the dogs are the athletes."[18]

At last, the long months of preparation were over. One April morning in 1983, Gary Paulsen nervously waited his turn at the starting gate of the Iditarod.

Dancing With Winter: The Iditarod

"It's not sane, and yet I would do the Iditarod until I die."[1]

For beginner Gary Paulsen, the start of the Iditarod in 1983 was a fiasco. He was informally voted "least likely to make it out of Anchorage," and it almost came true.[2] The town was crowded with people, sleds, and dogs. The frenzied sounds of snarls, dogfights, and yelling filled the air.

Pre-race jitters made him take Cookie off the lead position to protect her in the chaos. Not wanting her injured leaving the chute, he replaced her with Wilson, who, supposedly, had raced before. Only later did Paulsen learn that Wilson had no racing experience.

Mushers drew numbers for their start time. Paulsen was number thirty-two out of more than seventy teams. At his turn, he waited on the sled, rigid with fear.

Wilson shot from the chute two seconds early. Almost immediately, he missed a turn, careered through the crowd, plowed over garbage cans and ripped out fences. Like a video on fast-forward, it was a fearsome beginning for the life-and-death adventure ahead.[3]

The ceremonial start in Anchorage is for sponsors, fans, and reporters. A restart takes place later, past the freeway system of Anchorage. Paulsen's wife and

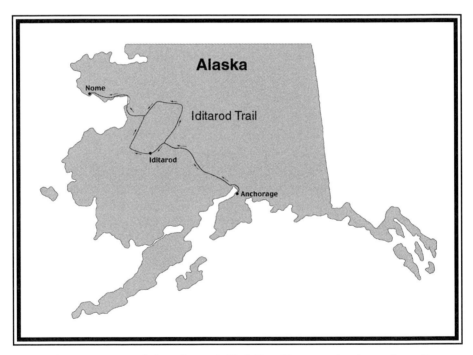

This overview of the Iditarod Sled Dog Race route shows how it loops north in even-numbered years, south in odd-numbered years. The Iditarod Trail is said to be 1,049 miles long. It is more than 1,000 miles, and the number 49 stands for Alaska, the 49th state.

the handlers met him outside Anchorage and piled the dogs into the trucks for the trip to the official start. Ruth Paulsen was afraid of what lay ahead for her husband.

With Cookie back in the lead, Paulsen and his dogs took off again in the late afternoon. Officials marked each musher's starting time. Right away there was trouble. Paulsen's sled flipped on its side then back up. He was dragged on the ground and his clothes were packed with snow. As he worked to clear out the snow, he did not notice when Cookie took a right fork instead of a left. By then it was dark.

Up a mountainside they zigzagged. Paulsen was wondering if this was some kind of test for rookies— and then the trail ran out. By the time he discovered that they had followed a snow machine track instead of the Iditarod Trail, they had run sixty miles in the wrong direction.

Worse, other teams had followed the scent of his dogs. Paulsen had to tell twenty-seven mushers that they must turn around. Dog teams growled and fought as they doubled back.

On the way back down, a moose lunged at him in the darkness. The six-hundred-pound beast missed Paulsen's dogs, but kicked him twice, and killed the lead dog of the team behind him before another musher shot the moose.

And that was only Day 1.

In the days that followed, Paulsen slept little. He fed meals and snacks to fifteen dogs, cared for their sixty paws, was knocked from his sled, and detoured around a buffalo. Once he had to feed all of his own food to one dog that had stopped eating. Paulsen was left with only butter for himself. At the next checkpoint, he ate nineteen servings of moose chili.

Despite his problems, the exquisite beauty of Alaska stunned Gary Paulsen. Everything was extremes—the terrain, the weather, the exhaustion. He slept little and cared endlessly for his dogs. Along the trail, he laughed and cried and talked out loud to ghostly hallucinations. He was awed by the savviness of his dogs.

When Paulsen saw the lights of Nome sparkling in the night sky, he almost turned back. He brought his team to a dead stop twenty miles from the end of the race, not wanting it to end.

He did not know that Ruth had gotten a ride from Nome in a Jeep so she could see him as he neared the finish of the arduous run. She and the driver watched as Paulsen's sled drew closer, then stopped.

When his wife called out to him, the sound of Ruth's voice broke the spell. Paulsen and the dogs drove on toward Nome, where a siren sounded, as it does when each team crosses the finish line. Paulsen was in tears as he embraced Ruth and their son, Jim.

Running the Iditarod had taken Paulsen seventeen days. Paulsen's dog team placed forty-second out of more than seventy teams, remarkable for a first-timer. Like all mushers who finished the race, Paulsen received an Iditarod belt buckle.

During the run, he took 750 slides and wrote in his journal, no matter how cold, hungry, or exhausted he felt. He was the first musher to document the

Paulsen and his dogs stop for a snooze along the Iditarod Trail.

Iditarod in that way. He later created a slide show of his best pictures.

Not only did Gary Paulsen run the Iditarod in 1983, he also had a book published with editor Richard Jackson. Jackson's trust in Paulsen had been well placed. As promised, Paulsen had sent the books he wrote to Jackson. In the first one, Paulsen built a story of hope and love around a man shattered by war. *Dancing Carl*, published in 1983, is based on a World War II veteran Paulsen had known as a boy. Carl dances out his love for a young woman at the town skating rink.

Dancing Carl touched many readers, reminding them of men like Carl who lived in their own hometowns.

Paulsen received hundreds of letters asking, "Is that our Carl?"

Despite his daring spirit, Paulsen was still shy with people. Making friends did not come easily for him. Just two months after the Iditarod, he attended his first large conference as a writer, an American Library Association meeting in Dallas, Texas.

Richard Jackson had arranged for Gary Paulsen to meet a few librarians at a small luncheon. Jarred and exhausted from the physical and mental stress of the Iditarod, he was also "nervous, confused, absolutely terrified that I would say or do something wrong," said Paulsen.[4]

Everyone at the lunch was pleasant. Still, Paulsen felt himself slipping away mentally. Then someone said, "I *loved* your book *Dancing Carl*. Tell me about it."[5] It was librarian Michael Printz.

Their friendship was almost instantaneous, as if they had always known each other. With his expertise in children's books, Mike Printz would become a sounding board, sometimes reading manuscripts before Paulsen sent them to publishers.

Recovering from the Iditarod, Gary Paulsen filled his days with running dogs and writing. He later wrote about his remarkable Iditarod adventures and his great love of dogs in five books: *Woodsong*, *Winterdance* (for adults), *Dogteam*, *My Life in Dog Years*, and *Puppies, Dogs, and Blue Northers*.

While training in Alaska in 1985 before his second Iditarod, Paulsen came close to a disaster. He started with a too-tight band for his head lamp and low batteries. He missed his dogs' restlessness and the hints of bad weather. Those mistakes could have killed him. The tight headband caused a throbbing headache, and he failed to sense signs of trouble.

With temperatures almost fifty degrees below zero, a sudden, blinding storm blew up. It seemed as if a white curtain had been drawn in front of him. In an instant, the dogs ahead of him disappeared from view. In winds more fierce than the typhoon he had experienced in the Philippines, he was torn sideways from the sled and tossed end-over-end down the mountain.

Thrown against some rocks, pinned there by the wind, Paulsen could barely move. His light was useless and it was only by sheer luck that he found his sled, not four feet away. The prongs of his snow hook had caught in a crack in some rocks. The rope from the snow hook to the dogs' gangline had held.

Paulsen could have stayed somewhat protected in a shallow hollow under an overhang. Instead, he fought his way out into the frigid winds to save his dogs, hoping against hope that the hook would hold.

One by one, he felt for harnesses, pulling dogs toward him. As a partial windbreak, he turned the sled on its side beneath the overhang. At last he huddled in his sleeping bag, piled dogs around him, and slept.

When daylight came, he was stunned by what he saw. The snow hook he had trusted the night before had shifted. Only the left prong now held a corner of rock. When Paulsen reached for it, the hook fell away. He found himself staring down into a deep canyon below—he and the dogs had been that close to death.[6]

Despite the numbing fear, Paulsen experienced

A snow hook like this one saved the lives of Paulsen and his dog team during a blinding Alaskan snowstorm. Attached to the dogs' gangline, the hook digs into the snow to keep a team from running while a musher rests or straightens a line.

another feeling. Freedom. The cold and the terror had brought with them a deep sense of liberation. He had found freedom in being completely alone. He also knew, without question, that he would run dogs as long as his life allowed.[7]

After his first Iditarod, Paulsen began raising and training Cookie's pups. In 1985, he was ready to run the Iditarod again, this time wanting to win. "That was sick," Paulsen later said bluntly.[8] Just eighty miles before the finish of the race in Nome, Alaska, he got lost.

The ice Paulsen and his team had been running

on broke loose. He was caught, adrift at sea on an ice floe, in a storm so ferocious that the winds blew his dogs over his head. They all floated on the floe for two days, shivering in the little shelter of a meager outcropping of ice. He knew that as the large ice floe melted, it was a matter of time before he and the dogs would die.

Again, luck was with him. A yellow bag on the sled would not stay tucked in. Miraculously, a bush pilot searching for him spotted the bright yellow and made a precarious landing on the ice in ninety-mile-per-hour winds.

"Are you Paulsen?" yelled the pilot.[9] Paulsen nodded. He cut lines and harnesses and began throwing dogs into the plane. The sled and all his equipment dropped away into frigid waters.

Paulsen had not quite made it aboard when the engine roared and winds gusted the plane up from the ice. With a death grip on a door handle, he was ninety feet in the air before he managed to haul himself inside the cabin.

The pilot shouted. The weight of the dogs at the back of the plane was causing it to founder. It would crash if he could not get the nose down. Paulsen had to move the dogs forward in a hurry.

During the whole perilous flight to Nome, Paulsen frantically tossed dogs toward the front to balance the weight. Terrified by the noise and rough ride, the dogs ripped at everything. Paulsen's feather parka was in shreds. They bit the pilot, they bit Paulsen—his hands still bear the scars. Before the twenty-one minute trip was over, the plane was filled with feathers, growls, barks, and blood.

The second running of the Iditarod proved to be another life-changing event for Gary Paulsen. "You're never normal again. Everything you do is measured against the Iditarod," Paulsen said.[10] For him the experiences were vital. In his writing, Paulsen has used many ideas that came to him in his twenty-two thousand miles of Alaskan dogsledding.

One book idea came from a chance meeting with a young Inuit boy during Paulsen's first Iditarod. At a checkpoint, the boy had asked him about his sled dogs. Paulsen was amazed to find himself, a white man from Minnesota, teaching a native Alaskan about sled dogs.

In his writer's mind, a plot grew. "What if an Eskimo boy used a dogteam to find himself?" he wondered.[11] *Dogsong* was born. In this book, an Eskimo boy who lives where snowmobiles and alcohol are smothering the culture wants to learn the old ways.

Dogsong was especially important in Paulsen's career. It became his first Newbery Honor Book, receiving one of the highest awards in children's literature. *Dogsong* won other honors, too, including being named Best Book for Young Adults for 1986 by the American Library Association.

With *Dogsong* came recognition. Paulsen began to do book signings and school visits. He wanted to know his readers. Instead of eating lunch in the teachers' lounge at schools, he sat with students in the cafeteria. He gained a clear picture of what young people wanted to know and read about.

Gary Paulsen toured widely, visiting as many as four schools a day across the country. "I went to

Paulsen continued running his dogs after his two experiences with the Iditarod, including this 1986 race in the wilderness of Minnesota.

Alaskan villages in a bush plane. I went to inner-city Detroit," said Paulsen.[12] Often he stretched the fees paid him by schools that could afford his visits to cover free visits to schools in poorer areas.

His goal was to reach "the kids who were like me, who didn't have a shot at it, whose folks were drunks, who lived on the outside of society."[13] When he found those students, Paulsen had frank, quiet talks with them about his life and their lives and what it was all about.

Two books that reflected Paulsen's strong antiwar feelings came next. *Sentries* was published in 1986, a year after *Dogsong*. From his own experience in the military and from knowing many veterans, Paulsen viewed war as senseless, a total waste of human lives. He saw *Sentries* as one of his most important works for young people.

Paulsen demands much from his readers in *Sentries*. Instead of using a standard plot in this challenging book, he introduces four teens searching for meaning in their lives. Between their tales, Paulsen weaves in four segments he calls battle hymns. He spares nothing in these stories of soldiers from three wars—Vietnam, Korea, and World War II.

In Paulsen's view, adults have made a mess of things. *Sentries* poses hard questions, but "I'm betting that young people have the answers," said Paulsen. He also painted an unglorified picture of the military in *The Crossing* (1987), drawing on experiences in Juárez, Mexico, while he was in the Army.[14]

Throughout his time of training dogs, running two Iditarods, and after, Paulsen filled every spare moment with writing. His persistence and hard work were paying off.

He was edging toward fame.

Hatchet!

"My life exploded."[1]

Then came *Hatchet.*

The backdrop for Paulsen's best-known book had long been a part of him, drawn from the deep bond with nature forged in his teens. In those troubled years, the woods, lakes, and rivers had provided both refuge and salvation. It was "on the soft winding rivers and quiet blue lakes, in the quick splash of fall color, the hiss of line going off a reel, the soft crack of an old .22 rifle sighted on grouse (fool hen), the shaking hands that aimed at first deer with a straight bow and homemade arrows—it was there that *Hatchet* was born," Paulsen later wrote.[2]

During National Library Week, in April 1986, Paulsen was on an author tour. When he walked into Hershey Middle School, in Hershey, Pennsylvania,

Gary Paulsen looks on as Hershey Middle School students add details to an Iditarod mural in 1986.

Paulsen sensed an energy—the whole school hummed. Hershey's students were fired up, thirsty for knowledge.[3] The teachers and administrators, too, were committed to all aspects of education, including the arts.[4]

Hershey's librarian, Mary Ann Achorn, was so excited when Gary Paulsen accepted her invitation to speak about the Iditarod that her enthusiasm spread. Students prepared by reading all the Paulsen books they could get their hands on and digging out details on the Iditarod. They pored over Iditarod maps, photos, and articles. Sixth graders made a mural, and race results from Alaska were announced over the loudspeaker. The school was *ready*.

The moment Paulsen entered the school, he felt their eagerness. While he showed his Iditarod slides, the magic of his storytelling transported Hershey students to the Alaskan run with its wind and cold, dangers and wonder, its dog songs. Then they peppered him with questions. "They were like pups—they just ripped and tore," he said.[5] Their keen interest bowled Paulsen over.

He knew then that it was time for the survival tale that had been brewing in his mind. The title would be, simply, *Hatchet*. Like the Hershey students, he went to work.

That summer, it was Hershey Middle School's turn to be surprised. Mary Ann Achorn received a package from Barbara Lalicki, Paulsen's editor, with news. Gary Paulsen had dedicated *Hatchet* "to a school he thinks is truly special."[6] Lalicki sent the school a set of bound galleys (a prepublication version) of the book and sketches for cover artwork done by Neil Waldman.

When *Hatchet* hit the bookstores, it just took off.

Millions of copies of *Hatchet* have been sold since 1987. Paulsen cannot explain why this book rocketed to popularity. It was, after all, a straight adventure story. Thirteen-year-old Brian Robeson has only a hatchet for survival after a plane crash in the Canadian wilderness. Brian struggles with hunger, illness, storms, wild animals, and mosquitoes.

The story goes deeper, though. *Hatchet* is layered with Brian's fears, insights, and growing appreciation of the natural world. With only himself to rely upon, he stumbles, learns, and grows. By the book's end, he is changed.

Like the character Brian, Paulsen had eaten raw turtle eggs ("pretty rank"), flown with bush pilots over the deep woods, and started a fire with a hatchet.[7] *Hatchet* holds strong appeal. The book makes readers ask themselves how they would think and act if stranded alone. What would they eat? How would they deal with bad weather or meeting a moose or a bear? Could they survive as Brian does?

The story is so realistic that Paulsen received phone calls from magazines interested in running stories on Brian Robeson. Some wanted to take Brian back to the deep Canadian north woods where he had survived alone for fifty-four days. Paulsen explained the hitch in their plans: Brian does not really exist— he is a fictional character.

Paulsen was taken aback by the book's explosive

Paulsen had already written many books by 1988 when Hatchet *was published.*

success. *Hatchet* remains one of the biggest-selling young adult books in history.

By now, Gary Paulsen was becoming well known. "All of a sudden, librarians and teachers were 'discovering' a guy who had already published fifty books," said reading expert Jim Trelease.[8] Paulsen's early days of scraping out a living were over.

In January 1988, Gary Paulsen received his second Newbery Honor award, this one for *Hatchet*. His editor, Barbara Lalicki, mailed Newbery Honor stickers to Hershey Middle School librarian Mary Ann Achorn and wrote, "Isn't it fun to have been there at the start?"[9] On a Monday in September, Hershey Middle School declared Gary Paulsen Day. The author was back, this time to officially dedicate *Hatchet* to the school's students. Neil Waldman, who did the cover art, went with him and the school buzzed with speeches and art projects. Local and state representatives attended the gala dedication. Student authors read their work, too, at the ceremony.

This event was tailor-made for writer Gary Paulsen—a lively celebration of books and young readers, librarians and educators, art and ideas.

More Risks,
More Books

"I could write, or I could run dogs. But I couldn't do both."[1]

As the sales of *Hatchet* soared, Paulsen's life was tinged with sadness. He experienced a double loss—a good friend, and his sled dogs.

Gary Paulsen's close friend and agent was dying. During his illness, the friend talked about all the things he had dreamed of doing in his life but now would never do. It made Paulsen think about his own life. What did he want to do in the time he had left on Earth?

He knew—he wanted to write.

Three years after his second Iditarod, Paulsen was still running his dogs for the joy and wonder of it. He often ran eighty miles in a day. Back home afterward, he would write for hours.

These days filled with dogsledding and writing caught up with him early in 1988. While on a run, one dog cut its foot. Kneeling to patch the wound and put on a bootie, Paulsen fell asleep, "BANG! I was so tired," he said.[2]

His dogs lay down and slept, too. Inches of snow covered Paulsen when he awoke two hours later. His hands had frostbite, and he could not move because his legs were numb. That accidental sleep could have caused his death. Nearing fifty, he no longer had the stamina needed to run dogs for fourteen hours and then write into the early morning.

Gary Paulsen felt it was time to give up running sled dogs. With a big book tour coming up, he sold his dogs to a friend for one dollar.[3] He kept only Cookie, his wise lead dog. Invited into the house to live, Cookie promptly ate Ruth Paulsen's cat.

Life had changed for the Paulsens. For the first time, the family had a washer, dryer, and all new furniture for a little home south of Bemidji, Minnesota. A converted hog barn became a spacious, light-filled artist's studio for Ruth.

Their son, Jim, who had planned to start college in the fall of 1988, announced that he was enlisting in the Army instead. Paulsen felt fear for his son, fury with the recruiter. Mike Printz, Paulsen's longtime friend, suggested that he find something Jim would rather do.[4] Gary offered him a bike trip in Europe. Jim, an avid cyclist, chose the trip over the Army. Something of Jim found its way into Paulsen's next book, *The Island*. Paulsen modeled the character of

Gary and Ruth Wright Paulsen in 1988 with their son, Jim, nicknamed Gito.

Wil on his son, and he dedicated the book to Mike Printz.

Paulsen's departure from dogsledding was temporary. A year and a half later he had dogs again—thirty-seven of them. Repeating the Iditarod was on his mind, perhaps in 1989 or 1990.

Always adventurous, Paulsen had sailed off and on since the mid-1960s. Once, he headed for Hawaii in a fiberglass sailboat just twenty-two feet long. He not only survived a harrowing storm in the Pacific, but later his small boat was surrounded by six orcas, black-and-white killer whales. Amazed, Paulsen wondered if he looked to them like "a big, juicy pork chop."[5] For *The Voyage of the Frog*, 1989, about self-reliance and facing death, he blended experiences from his many sailing trips into the plot.

Paulsen composed his next book, *The Winter Room*, 1989, as a symphony while he and Ruth were listening to music by Austrian composer Gustav Mahler. A reflection on the seasons, it weaves winter storytelling with memory and a search for truth. The book was named Paulsen's third Newbery Honor Book in 1990.

When Cookie died peacefully on September 10, 1989, Paulsen mourned her death. To him, she was more than a dog. In speeches around the country he has said she was more like a "sisterdog" or a sister. Cookie "saved my life—three times that I know of, maybe more that I wasn't aware of," said Paulsen.[6] He buried Cookie's #32 metal tag from the Iditarod with her and dedicated *Woodsong* to her.

While touring in 1990, sudden fierce chest pains

dropped Paulsen to his knees in Boston's Logan Airport. He made it back home, where he was diagnosed with heart disease. He looked at death and knew its coppery taste. "Then the hardest thing of all—the phone call to a friend: 'You have to come and take them all—pups, dogs, sleds.'"[7] He knew that they had to be gone before he returned home from the hospital.

With the time of long, joyous dog runs over for good, Paulsen found an eighteen-hour hole in his days. He filled it with writing. He learned to use a word processor and even began to enjoy rewriting. Sometimes he went back and opened the computer files of already published books to see how he could have written them differently.

Gary Paulsen's life now centered on writing books and reaching his avid fans. From the mid-1980s on, he had toured—talking about the Iditarod, his books, and writing. He was still speaking widely, delighting in the response of his readers.

Once Paulsen was on a panel at a Minnesota college when a swarm of students from a nearby middle school burst in. Paulsen said later that they had "commandeered a bus somehow and crashed this thing! Everybody had been so proper before, and the kids just blew it wide open!"[8] The students poured out questions about *Hatchet*, *Dogsong*, and Paulsen's other books.

To make time for writing, he began to cut down on his touring schedule. Three Paulsen books, with three different styles, were published in 1990—the reflective

Canyons, the comical *The Boy Who Owned the School*, and *Woodsong*.

Woodsong takes readers into the rawness and beauty of the natural world and includes a day-by-day record of Paulsen's first Iditarod race. Librarian Mike Printz called the book "Gary's autobiographical story concerning his life with his dogs and life and death."[9]

A former student of Printz's had avidly read Paulsen's books. Now hospitalized with a serious illness, the young man eagerly borrowed a prepublication copy of *Woodsong* from Printz. When Printz returned the next day for another visit, this young friend looked Printz in the eye and said, "I'm not scared anymore."[10] Once again, Paulsen had connected powerfully with a reader at a crucial moment.

Paulsen's next book, *The Monument*, featured a girl in the lead role. It was dedicated to his father, whom Gary came to know better in the last seven years of the older man's life. Paulsen never did become close to his mother, who had died earlier.[11]

Brian Robeson, the *Hatchet* character, returned in 1991 in *The River*, to teach his skills to a government psychologist studying survival skills.

In 1992, Paulsen was excited about a new series called Culpepper Adventures. A man had once told Paulsen that the first book he read in his whole life was *Hatchet*, and the first letter he ever wrote was to his adult son urging him to read it, too.

This pushed Paulsen to write page-turners, slim paperback books designed to hook young readers. Fast-paced and funny, they feature Dunc Culpepper and Amos Binder, dubbed "friends for life" by the author. They solve mysteries, travel through time, and have other wild adventures.

In one Culpepper Adventure, Paulsen added an inside joke. Amos tries unsuccessfully to use a book called *Hatchet* for tips when he is caught in the wilderness. Paulsen hoped this series, with six Culpepper books added each year, would help launch students' love of reading.

To keep pace with his writing plans, Paulsen still wrote every day, but 1992 was an unsettled time. He and his wife were traveling back and forth between New Mexico and Minnesota, deciding where to settle permanently. Ruth Paulsen's skills as an artist continued to grow, and she was exhibiting her artwork throughout the Midwest.

Diet and exercise had helped ease Gary Paulsen's heart problems, but his physical activities were still limited. Always adventurous, he found a new way to explore the wilds—on horseback in Wyoming.

Two horses named Merry and Blackie took him places in Wyoming's Big Horn Mountains where he could not have gone on foot. Riding Merry, with Blackie packing his supplies, Paulsen felt the ghosts at the site of Custer's Last Stand, gave bears the slip, fell down a mountain, and was caught in a flash flood. He also saw "sunsets and dawns that no man, ever, has seen before or will see again in the same way or place."[12] Many of these experiences were used in his book *The Haymeadow*, published in 1992.

A February visit back to Minnesota, where the temperatures were close to fifty degrees below zero,

If he writes about it, he has tried it. Outdoorsman Gary Paulsen is just as comfortable surviving in the wilderness as he is creating stories at the computer keyboard.

convinced Paulsen that without the fun of running dogs, the winters there were too cold. The Paulsens made a permanent move to New Mexico, with their horses in tow.

After years of focusing primarily on writing for children, Paulsen said, "I started hitting these walls. There'd be things I wanted to write about and I couldn't, because they would have to fit in a young person's world. It was almost like a new medium, like going from pastels to oils."[13] He had written a collection of short stories for adults in 1989. Now he published two adult books in two years. Both *Eastern Sun, Winter Moon: An Autobiographical Odyssey* and *Clabbered Dirt, Sweet Grass* were grounded in his life experiences.

The year 1993 was a record breaker even for the prolific Paulsen. Besides more Culpepper books, he published four books: *Harris and Me: A Summer Remembered,* with its deadpan humor; *Sisters/Hermanas,* about two fourteen-year-old girls, one a prostitute and one a cheerleader; *Dogteam;* and *Nightjohn.*

Many of Paulsen's books arise from his experiences. Others, like *Nightjohn,* blend experience with research. Paulsen had discovered firsthand accounts of the lives of slaves. "I sat in my basement reading these [slave chronicles] crying every night," said Paulsen.[14] In five years of research, he found that slaves who tried to learn to read could be killed. Still they persisted—learning, then teaching others by reading letters taken from the big house or pages of mail-order catalogs.

Because slaves were valuable, a master might prefer not to kill a slave for breaking the rule. Instead, the slave's thumb or a toe would be cut off as punishment. "Most of the owners were terrified of the slaves learning to read, because they knew they would want to be free," said Paulsen.[15]

Paulsen had taught himself to read. He knew how the slave called *Nightjohn* could help twelve-year-old Sarny figure out that letters formed of lines and circles in the dirt could make meaning. The knowledge that comes from reading is at the core of *Nightjohn*, and the plot is rooted in the true stories of slaves.

Paulsen's adventures continued. In his lifetime, he had owned many different "rides," from motor-powered bicycles to motorcycles, and he had broken many bones—arm, leg, wrist, ankle. But when he bought a Harley-Davidson motorcycle in 1993, the sound and the fit swept him away. With a friend, Paulsen, now fifty-four, rode from New Mexico to Fairbanks, Alaska, and back, in just twelve days. Some days they covered seven hundred miles.

Despite close calls—hitting a big seagull dead-on, wheels caught in a road groove, bad falls—the Harley took Paulsen on the ride of his life.

The Fine Madness of Writing

"I write the same way I live—absolutely to the firewall."[1]

Paulsen still loved dogsledding, even though the Iditarod was now a thing of the past and he lived in New Mexico. In January 1994, Paulsen made a winter trip to Michigan's Upper Peninsula, where a friend was preparing for the Iditarod.[2] Warm in a fur-lined parka, he relished his short runs. Gleefully he commanded, "On by! On by!" to the eager sled dogs.[3]

Details of sledding and the Iditarod came through in Paulsen's adult book *Winterdance: The Fine Madness of Running the Iditarod*, published in 1994. Paulsen based it on his more than twenty thousand miles of Alaskan dogsledding. For another 1994 book, *The Car*, he assembled a kit car called a Blakely Bearcat and drove it on a trip. A revised version of his first young adult book, *Mr. Tucket*, also came out that year.

Everywhere Paulsen went, he wrote—in hotel rooms, waiting to meet people, while flying. He wrote in small spiral notebooks, in journals, or on his laptop computer. "I've learned to map out a whole book in my head before I even start to write it," he said.[4]

From his autobiographical *Father Water, Mother Woods*, readers learned more about the hunting, fishing, and camping that had eased Paulsen's painful teen years. Ruth Wright Paulsen illustrated the book.

Now Gary Paulsen was ready to hook older students on reading, as his Culpepper books had snagged younger ones. He started the Gary Paulsen World of Adventure series in 1994, writing the paperbacks quickly and packing them with action. Plots include sky diving, high-tech computer games, sunken treasures, mind control, and more. Paulsen hoped that preteens and teens would dive into those fast-moving stories instead of watching TV.[5]

Paulsen received the Jeremiah Ludington Award in 1994 for his significant contributions to the world of children's paperbacks.[6] He also signed a multibook contract with Harcourt Brace and Company.

In the summer of 1994, Paulsen lived on his thirty-eight-foot sloop *Felicity* in a marina in Ventura, California. He was repairing the boat, getting ready for more sailing adventures and writing on his laptop computer.

The desperate money worries of a decade earlier were over. "I've never been a successful financial person and now I kinda am. Suddenly I'm one of those

"The boat is one of my favorite places to write," says Paulsen, *onboard* Felicity.

people who could play *golf*," said Paulsen, slightly horrified. "But I'm not like that. I just work. I believe in what I do, and I just work."[7] He found ways to use his money, supporting a Russian orphanage with royalty payments from Russian translations of his books, sponsoring dogsledders, and rescuing dogs from the local pound.[8]

Paulsen kept up his furious writing pace. Besides adding new titles to his two series in 1995, he also published four other books: *The Rifle, The Tent, The Tortilla Factory* (a picture book with Ruth Wright Paulsen's rich illustrations), and *Call Me Francis Tucket*.

The Rifle follows a weapon from its creation by a master gunsmith before the Revolutionary War to current times. Reviewer Jean Patrick said, "You may dismiss *The Rifle* as the story of a freak accident. More likely, you'll be haunted by the deadly potential of guns."[9] He received the Regina Medal, a lifetime achievement award, from the Catholic Library Association in 1995.

Puppies, Dogs, and Blue Northers, published in 1996, is Cookie's story. Illustrated by Ruth Wright Paulsen, it is a book about love. Gary Paulsen marvels at Cookie and all of his dogs—their intelligence, fierce loyalty, tricks, and sweetness. "It is impossible not to love them, even when they are eating your favorite parka," said Paulsen.[10]

As Paulsen's popularity grew, he began getting more and more mail—two hundred letters or more every day. Fans asked about Brian Robeson. What happened to him? What if he had not been rescued by wintertime? Paulsen had begun to wonder that himself.

The time had come to write again about Brian Robeson. Gary Paulsen knew about winter survival. He had hunted and trapped in winter and run two grueling Iditarods.

In the opening of the new book, *Brian's Winter*, Paulsen conspires with his readers to change the ending of *Hatchet*. He stresses that Brian could not have survived if the plane had first crashed in winter. But Brian could have built on the survival skills he had already learned. Then Paulsen asks readers to set aside two key events from *Hatchet*—Brian's triggering the radio signal and his rescue.

In *Brian's Winter*, readers feel the battering by a bear, the poignant humor of his friendship with a skunk, and the terror of thinking that trees exploding in the deep cold are gunshots. Paulsen's readers grow as Brian grows.

At the end of *Brian's Winter*, they understand Brian's mix of joy and regret when rescue is near. The character Brian asks the same questions Gary Paulsen had asked himself many times: How can I leave this solitary beauty? How can I be in the world again?

Gary Paulsen's longtime friend Mike Printz died in 1996. He had nurtured many writers and loved Paulsen's work. Printz had stood by Paulsen as both a fan and a friend. It was Printz who had talked him through his fears about his heart problems. After the librarian's death, friends wrote a collection of essays

Paulsen speaks to eager young readers at Books & Co. in Dayton, Ohio. Crowds of enthusiastic fans poured into bookstores to meet Paulsen as he toured the country for Brian's Winter.

celebrating the life of Michael Printz. Paulsen titled his contribution simply "My Favorite Fan."[11]

Mike Printz, wrote Paulsen, was a man who "truly loved books. Loved the paper, loved the ink, the covers, even the process and that love extended in some wonderful way to the authors."[12]

In that same way, Gary Paulsen was hooking readers so they could celebrate words and be in love with books. Reading, Paulsen knew, could enrich and change their lives.

He asks something of his readers. In an essay called "Tuning" in *The Winter Room*, he wrote, "If books could be more, could show more, could own more, this book would have . . . sound and smell and light and all the rest that can't be in books. The book needs you."[13]

"Without [readers] we're nothing," said Paulsen. "We're really nothing without that bond, that incredible intimacy. I think it's almost sacred that a person will allow you into their mind through a book."[14]

Paulsen still relished memories of his twelve-day, round-trip ride to Alaska on a Harley, another extreme adventure for him. In 1997, he published an adult book about it, *Pilgrimage on a Steel Ride*, mixing earlier memories with tales of perils met on the road. The writing was started on his fifty-seventh birthday, after a sailing adventure in Mexico's Sea of Cortés. Between making repairs on an old sailboat in a California marina, he had worked on the book.

Young adult librarians honored Gary Paulsen in 1997 with the Margaret A. Edwards Award from the American Library Association (ALA) for his lifetime contribution in writing books for teens. The ALA cited six of Paulsen's books: *Dancing Carl*, *Hatchet*, *The Crossing*, *The Winter Room*, *Woodsong*, and *Canyons*. Helen Vandersluis of the ALA said, "His writing conveys a profound respect for [young adults'] intelligence and ability to overcome life's worst realities."[15]

In his acceptance speech, Paulsen told of the librarian of his youth who had seen past his toughness and touched his heart. "When she handed me a library card," he said, "she handed me the world."[16]

His work output was increasing. Essays on Cookie, ice fishing, and dogsledding appeared in *Reader's Digest*, the *Lands' End* catalog, and other

Paulsen signs books in San Francisco after receiving the 1997 Margaret A. Edwards Award for his lifetime contribution to young adult literature.

publications. *Worksong*, a 1997 picture book with Ruth Wright Paulsen's illustrations, celebrates unsung heroes, workers who keep steadily at their jobs day after day. More audiotapes of his books became available.

Paulsen thinks of himself "as a chronicler. I think in feelings, emotions, and the sweep of life."[17] That sweep shows in *Soldier's Heart*, published in 1998. Based on a real person, the book frames the Civil War through the eyes of Charley Goddard, an underage soldier who enlists to serve in the First Minnesota Volunteers.

Today the psychological wounds of war are labeled *shell shock*, *combat fatigue*, or *post-traumatic stress disorder*. At the time of the Civil War, this wound to soldiers' minds and souls was simply called "soldier's heart."

Wendy Lamb, Paulsen's editor at Delacorte Press, had a special connection to the book. The discharge document for Isaac Babbitt, her great-grandfather, who ran away to enlist as a drummer boy at age fifteen, is used on the cover of *Soldier's Heart*. For occupation, a clerk had written in the fancy copperplate handwriting of the time, "Boy."[18] That fit Charley Goddard perfectly. Charley did survive, but the war had marked him—he died at age twenty-three.

Paulsen wrote *My Life in Dog Years* while he was on a sailing trip along the coast of British Columbia in Canada. The book, which was published in 1998, celebrates Paulsen's lifetime as a "dog person."

His unabashed love for dogs comes through in his

essays on Snowball, Quincy, and others. Pen-and-ink drawings by Ruth Wright Paulsen grace the chapters, capturing each dog's look and personality.

In August 1998, Paulsen ran aground on a reef while sailing. As his boat was being repaired on one of the islands of Fiji in the South Pacific Ocean, he was back working "like a whirling dervish on books," said his agent, Jennifer Flannery. "That's all that's really new in his life—new books and problems with the boat."[19]

The eagerly awaited *Brian's Return*, the fourth story in his survival series about Brian Robeson, came out in 1999. It was to have been the last in the Brian series, but during a monthlong book tour in March 1999, so many readers begged to know what happened next to Brian, that Paulsen is contemplating two more books. One will be nonfiction, about the parallels between Brian's adventures and Paulsen's real-life ones. The other would be another novel about Brian.

Also published in 1999 were three books. One was *Alida's Song*, about his fourteenth summer, spent on a farm with Alida Moen, his beloved and steadfast grandmother. The others were *Canoe Days*, a picture book, and *Tucket's Gold*.

Away from the limelight, it is only Paulsen and the page. "It's almost like a dance," he said. "I think writing is really, really primitive—wearing bloody skins, dancing around the fire trying to tell what the hunt was like."[20]

He says he is "totally, viciously, obsessively committed to work, the way I'd run dogs. . . . I still work

Gary Paulsen with Josh in 1997, the year before they appeared on the cover of My Life in Dog Years. *"I have always had dogs and will have dogs until I die," says Paulsen.*

that way, completely, all the time. I just work. I don't drink, I don't fool around, I'm just this way."[21]

And write he does. He wakes around 5:30 each morning, has tea, meditates, and begins his writing day. Classical music plays in the background. At home, he enjoys a spectacular view of a mountain range. At sea, ever changing vistas greet him. Rather than wrestle with the how of writing, he works instinctively, matching tone with character and situation.

The way into *Dogsong* was through poetry; the way into *Hatchet* was through action. Occasionally he uses one long sentence, pulling readers along. For Paulsen, such sentences say, "Let's do this run, let's go down this long hill together."[22]

Sometimes, outraged at what humans are doing to the planet and its inhabitants, Paulsen roars.[23] He does not flinch from dark topics—the injustice of slavery, a deer viciously killed by wolves, or the realities of a rough childhood like his own. "Fortunately for all of us, Gary Paulsen has had the courage to risk censure [criticism] in order to tell a powerful story in a style only he is capable of," wrote one admiring critic.[24]

Paulsen stands behind his truth telling: "So much that's told to children is not based on truth. . . . There's a widespread, misguided attempt to protect [them]. Kids have to know about AIDS, for instance, if they're going to be able to fight it."[25] About television, he has said bluntly, "Television is an abomination—it actually causes a reversal in intelligence."[26]

The self-importance of humans "has become something close to horrific . . . [and has] ultimately led to such monstrosities as death camps and genocide, which are really nothing more than an insanely rabid expression of one race thinking they are superior to another," he has said.[27]

Fans like his frankness. Their messages to him move Paulsen to laughter or tears. He has been told that thinking too hard about books has made him bald, or that his book jacket picture makes him look old. One boy said he thought books were boring, but since he read *Hatchet*, "I might start reading books now."[28]

A boys' book club posted an Internet message about a feast they concocted after reading *Hatchet*. They ate "foolbirds" (grilled whole chicken), raspberries, and "turtle" eggs (deviled eggs), as Brian had in *Hatchet*.[29] Once, a ten-year-old concert pianist sent a tape of music he had written for one of Paulsen's books. Sometimes young people share problems they are having. Paulsen takes those letters very seriously.

For Paulsen, communication is a two-way street. He responds, often with a computer letter that he updates weekly. Readers can visit his Web site <www.randomhouse.com/features/garypaulsen/> to learn of his latest adventures. In the spring of 1999, these included sailing from Fiji, ripping off the rudders of his catamaran (a type of sailboat—cat, for short) near the islands of Tonga, repairing his damaged cat in shark-infested waters. He was turning in more book manuscripts written at sea on his laptop computer and visiting many bookstores.

In contrast to his own troubled childhood, Paulsen's family is strong. Gary and Ruth Paulsen have collaborated on many projects. Sometimes

Paulsen visits the White Rabbit Children's Bookstore in La Jolla, California, during a tour for Brian's Return *in 1999.*

Paulsen slips into his wife's studio while she works to watch "the miracle of starting with just a line. . . . I wouldn't have any soft edges without her," he has said.[30] He is visibly proud of his three grown children and of his grandchildren.

Gary Paulsen is most comfortable in his trademark jeans and suspenders. With his hearty laugh and broad smile, Paulsen is full of life. When not writing, he rides horses, lectures, and sails. He still dreams of heading south from Alaska and sailing around Cape Horn in South America, then back north to Chesapeake Bay on the East Coast of the United States.

More books are sure to come from such adventures.

Gary Paulsen's Legacy

"To be able to portray things I see and hear in writing is a privilege."[1]

Gary Paulsen is an adventurer, a romantic, a risk taker, and a passionate spokesman for the earth and its inhabitants. Like Brian Robeson of *Hatchet*, Paulsen knows what gives meaning to his life. Most important are his family, the natural world, and writing—always the writing.

Humor, adventure, survival, history, mystery, and memoir—Paulsen can do it all. As a writer, he explores new styles, stretching and growing. His work ranges from gentle to gritty, sidesplitting to somber. He has successfully mined his life and the world at large for writing ideas. Every day, he writes—his writing consumes him. Justice, often tempered with funny-bone humor, frames his work.

From the hard times while growing up, Paulsen

learned self-reliance. Against tremendous odds he has become a prolific writer. Paulsen has written more than two hundred books. His work has been translated into fifteen languages, and more than 15 million copies of his books are in print.[2]

With three Newbery Honor Books and many other prestigious honors and awards, his popularity still surprises him: "I'm not the kind of person this happens to," said Paulsen.[3]

From grade school students to adults, Paulsen pulls in readers. He remembers what it is like to be a child and a teenager. He knows and understands young people's feelings and emotions. In libraries, Gary Paulsen books fly off the shelves, and crowds flock to his book signings and lectures. Writer Theodore Taylor has called Paulsen "the best YA [young adult] writer on the planet."[4]

Despite this wide recognition, Paulsen remains rooted. With characteristic modesty, he says, "Fame has never really impressed me with its permanency."[5] The poverty of his early years keeps him humble. The well-remembered problems give him empathy.

Many of Paulsen's book titles include the word *song* or *dance*. In the same way, Paulsen's words dance on the page and his books sing their themes: knowing yourself, the importance of creativity and the arts, the horror and futility of war, and a love of reading.

Paulsen is passionate about reading. All knowledge, he has said, "is locked up in books, and if you can't read, it's lost."[6] Surefooted and driven, Gary Paulsen has left his distinct mark on the field of

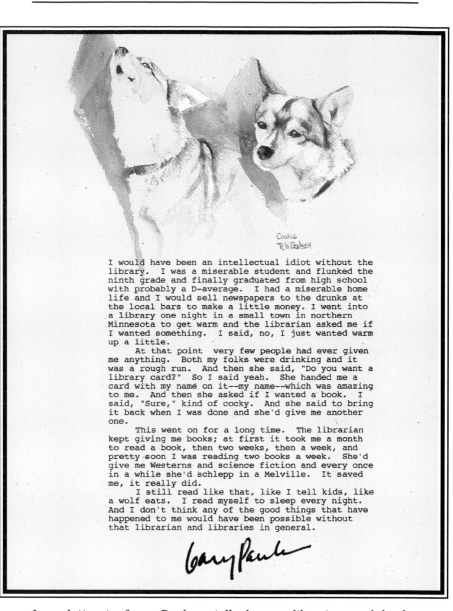

Cookie
R W Paulsen

I would have been an intellectual idiot without the library. I was a miserable student and flunked the ninth grade and finally graduated from high school with probably a D-average. I had a miserable home life and I would sell newspapers to the drunks at the local bars to make a little money. I went into a library one night in a small town in northern Minnesota to get warm and the librarian asked me if I wanted something. I said, no, I just wanted warm up a little.

At that point very few people had ever given me anything. Both my folks were drinking and it was a rough run. And then she said, "Do you want a library card?" So I said yeah. She handed me a card with my name on it--my name--which was amazing to me. And then she asked if I wanted a book. I said, "Sure," kind of cocky. And she said to bring it back when I was done and she'd give me another one.

This went on for a long time. The librarian kept giving me books; at first it took me a month to read a book, then two weeks, then a week, and pretty soon I was reading two books a week. She'd give me Westerns and science fiction and every once in a while she'd schlepp in a Melville. It saved me, it really did.

I still read like that, like I tell kids, like a wolf eats. I read myself to sleep every night. And I don't think any of the good things that have happened to me would have been possible without that librarian and libraries in general.

Gary Paulsen

In a letter to fans, Paulsen tells how a librarian and books changed his life. Ruth Wright Paulsen painted the two views of Cookie on her husband's stationery.

children's writing and beyond. Editor Wendy Lamb has said, "It's worked out brilliantly—a combination of his gifts with his work capacity and drive."[7]

From the Iditarod, Paulsen learned that "you can't stop, no matter what," and he cannot stop writing.[8] There is no danger that this amazing storyteller will run out of ideas. He has said he is "probably a hundred books behind."[9]

Today, even though Paulsen is still very active and follows a vegetarian diet, always on the edge of his mind is his heart disease. Instead of racing against snow and ice as he did in his dogsledding days, now he races against time.

Paulsen's great skill lies in linking young readers with books. Just as the librarian of his youth reached him, he has reached hundreds of thousands of students who might not otherwise read. He tells them to "read what they tell you not to read, and read when they tell you not to read. Read all the time."[10] He urges young people to be ravenous in their reading, and at public appearances he often wears a cap with the words "Read Like a Wolf Eats."

In turn, there's a hunger to his work. Not knowing how much time he has left, Gary Paulsen *writes* like a wolf eats.

(A selected list of Gary Paulsen's books is found on pages 112–114.)

1939—Born in Minneapolis, Minnesota, on May 17.

1944—Spends the summer with his grandmother at a cookcamp in northern Minnesota.

1945—The Paulsens live in the Philippines after World War II.

1953—Gets first library card.

1957—Graduates (barely) from Lincoln High School in Thief River Falls, Minnesota.

1959—Fails college and joins the Army; marries and has two children.

1962—Is discharged from the Army; finds a job tracking satellites in California; divorces.

1965—Decides to become a writer; moves to Hollywood.

1966—Returns alone to northern Minnesota. Sells two works, *Some Birds Don't Fly* (adult) and first book for young readers, *Mr. Tucket.*

1967—Problems with alcohol.
–1973

1969—Meets Ruth Ellen Wright.

1971—Marries Ruth Ellen Wright; son, Jim, born late that year.

1973—Stops drinking; has trouble getting back into
–1975   writing.

1976—Lives in poverty in Colorado.

1979—Returns to Minnesota.

1980—Is given four sled dogs.

1981—Makes a magical run across Clearwater Lake.

1983—Runs the Iditarod dogsled race in Alaska.

1985—Runs second Iditarod; is airlifted to safety from an ice floe near Nome.

1986—*Dogsong*, based on an Iditarod experience, is named a Newbery Honor Book.

1987—*Hatchet* is published.

1988—*Hatchet* is named a Newbery Honor Book.

1989—Cookie, Paulsen's lead dog, dies.

1990—*The Winter Room* is named a Newbery Honor Book.

1991—Moves to New Mexico.

1992—Starts the Culpepper Adventure series; travels between Minnesota and New Mexico, and into Wyoming.

1993—Rides Harley-Davidson motorcycle from New Mexico to Alaska.

1994—Starts Gary Paulsen World of Adventure series; restores an old sailboat in a California marina.

1995—Receives the Regina Medal, Catholic Library Association.

1997—Receives Margaret A. Edwards Award from the American Library Association.

1998—Publishes more books in his Culpepper Adventures and World of Adventure series books, plus *Soldier's Heart*, and others.

1999—Has published more than two hundred books, including *Brian's Return*, *Alida's Song*, *Tucket's Gold*, and *Canoe Days*; continues to sail, visit bookstores, and write prolifically.

Books by Gary Paulsen

Gary Paulsen says that most of his books, both fiction and nonfiction, are based on his life.

Selected Books for Young People

Nonfiction

Woodsong, 1990, based on his experiences in the natural world, training dogs, and running the Iditarod

Dogteam, 1993, a picture book based on Paulsen's love of dogsledding

Father Water, Mother Woods (young adult), 1994, essays based on his teen years spent hunting, fishing, and camping

Puppies, Dogs, and Blue Northers: Reflections on Being Raised by a Pack of Sled Dogs, 1996, about Cookie

My Life in Dog Years, 1998, short stories about his favorite dogs

Fiction

Tracker, 1984, based on twelve-year-old Gary's touching a deer

Hatchet, 1987, a Newbery Honor Book, based on his survival experiences

The Voyage of the Frog, 1989, based on his sailing adventures

The Winter Room, 1989, a Newbery Honor Book, based on Gary's childhood winters

Tiltawhirl John, 1990, based on his runaway summer

The Cookcamp, 1991, based on four-year-old Gary's summer with his grandmother in a northern Minnesota cookcamp

A Christmas Sonata, 1992, based on five-year-old Gary's Christmas with relatives

Harris and Me: A Summer Remembered, 1993, based on living with his relatives on their farms

Alida's Song, 1999, based on fourteen-year-old Gary's summer with his grandmother

Other books by Gary Paulsen

The Night the White Deer Died, 1978

The Foxman, 1978

Dancing Carl, 1983

Popcorn Days and Buttermilk Nights, 1983

Dogsong, 1985, a Newbery Honor Book

Sentries, 1986

The Crossing, 1987

The Island, 1988

Woodsong, 1990

The Boy Who Owned the School, 1990

Canyons, 1990

The Monument, 1991

The River, 1991

The Haymeadow, 1992

Nightjohn, 1993

Sisters / Hermanas, 1993

The Car, 1994

Mr. Tucket, revised edition, 1994
The Rifle, 1995
The Tent, 1995
Brian's Winter, 1996
Sarny: A Life Remembered, 1977
The Schernoff Discoveries, 1997
Soldier's Heart, 1998
Brian's Return, 1999

Chapter Notes

Chapter 1. A Mystical Run

1. Rich Davis, "Dog Sleds and Iditarod Fuel Author's Sense of Adventure," *The Evansville* [Indiana] *Courier*, March 8, 1992, p. F5.

2. Ibid.

3. Kay Miller, "Suddenly Fame and Fortune," *Star Tribune Sunday Magazine* (Minneapolis, Minn.), July 10, 1988, p. 11.

4. Alice Cary, *BookPage*, March 1994, p. 18.

5. "Kids on Paulsen," comments from letters to Gary Paulsen, courtesy of Jennifer Flannery, Flannery Literary.

Chapter 2. Childhood: At Home and Abroad

1. Gary Paulsen, *Eastern Sun, Winter Moon: An Autobiographical Odyssey* (New York: Harcourt Brace Jovanovich, 1993), p. 135.

2. Gary M. Salvner, *Presenting Gary Paulsen* (New York: Twayne Publishers, 1966), p. 7.

3. Paulsen, p. 4.

4. Ibid., p. 22.

5. Salvner, p. 9.

6. Paulsen, p. 96.

7. Ibid., p. 98.

8. Ibid., p. 113.

Chapter 3. Three Years in the Philippines

1. Gary Paulsen, *Eastern Sun, Winter Moon: An Autobiographical Odyssey* (New York: Harcourt Brace Jovanovich, 1993), p. 115.

2. Ibid., p. 132.

3. Gary Paulsen, *My Life in Dog Years* (New York: Delacorte Press), 1998, p. 14.

4. Paulsen, *Eastern Sun, Winter Moon*, p. 236.

5. Paulsen, *My Life in Dog Years*, p. 17.

6. Ibid., p. 18.

7. Paulsen, *Eastern Sun, Winter Moon*, p. 161.

8. Ibid., p. 123.

Chapter 4. The Runaway Years

1. Gary Paulsen, acceptance speech for Margaret A. Edwards Award from the American Library Association, San Francisco, June 28, 1997.

2. Mary Ann Grossmann, "Author Gary Paulsen Draws Upon His Own Wilderness Experiences," *Saint Paul* [Minn.] *Pioneer Press*, March 1996, p. 9D.

3. Holly Myers, *Elliott Bay Booknotes*, Fall 1993, p. 9.

4. Cheryl Bartky, "Write What You Are," *Writer's Digest*, July 1994, p. 42.

5. Gary Paulsen, *My Life in Dog Years* (New York: Delacorte Press, 1998), p. 34.

6. Sharon L. McElmeel, *Educator's Companion to Children's Literature, Volume 1: Mysteries, Animal Tales, Books of Humor, Adventure Stories, and Historical Fiction* (Englewood, Colo.: Teacher Ideas Press, 1995), p. 106.

7. Rich Davis, "Dog Sleds and Iditarod Fuel Author's Sense of Adventure," *The Evansville* [Indiana] *Courier*, March 8, 1992, p. F5.

8. Alice Evans Handy, "An Interview with Gary Paulsen," *The Book Report*, May/June 1991, p. 28.

9. Telephone interview with Jennifer Flannery, Flannery Literary, March 25, 1998.

10. Gary Paulsen, *Father Water, Mother Woods: Essays on Fishing and Hunting in the North Woods* (New York: Bantam Doubleday Dell Books for Young Readers, 1994), p. xii.

11. Gary Paulsen, letter to his fans, from Jennifer Flannery, Flannery Literary, December 2, 1997.

12. *Something About the Author* (Detroit, Mich.: Gale Research Inc., 1995), vol. 79, p. 162.

13. McElmeel, p. 106.

14. Paulsen, *My Life in Dog Years*, pp. 40–41.

15. Ibid., p. 46.

16. Gary Paulsen, speaking at a book signing at the White Rabbit Children's Books, La Jolla, Calif., May 5, 1999.

17. Ibid.

18. Gary Paulsen, *Pilgrimage on a Steel Ride* (New York: Harcourt Brace, 1997), p. 66.

19. Ibid., p. 67.

20. Ibid., p. 68.

21. Handy, p. 31.

Chapter 5. Bad Times

1. Kay Miller, "Suddenly Fame and Fortune," *Star Tribune Sunday Magazine* (Minneapolis, Minn.), July 10, 1988, p. 10.

2. Gary Paulsen, speaking at a book signing at the White Rabbit Children's Books, La Jolla, Calif., May 5, 1999.

3. Allen Raymond, "Artist-With-Words," *Teaching K-8*, August/September 1992, p. 54.

4. Gary Paulsen, *Pilgrimage on a Steel Ride* (New York: Harcourt Brace, 1997), pp. 12–13.

5. Holly Myers, *Elliott Bay Booknotes*, Fall 1993, p. 9.

6. Elizabeth Devereaux, "Gary Paulsen," *Publishers Weekly*, March 28, 1994, p. 70.

7. Ibid.

8. Raymond, p. 54.

9. Ibid.

10. Miller, p. 8.

11. *Something About the Author*, p. 80.

Chapter 6. Paulsen's Life as a Dog

1. Gary Paulsen, *Woodsong* (New York: Bradbury Press, 1990), p. 20.

2. Kay Miller, "Suddenly Fame and Fortune," *Star Tribune Sunday Magazine* (Minneapolis, Minn.), July 10, 1988, p. 11.

3. Ibid.

4. Adam Grant, "Dog Life," *Scholastic Scope,* January 26, 1996, p. 17.

5. Ibid., p. 18.

6. Gary Paulsen, speaking at a book signing at the White Rabbit Children's Books, La Jolla, Calif., May 5, 1999.

7. Grant, p. 18.

8. Paulsen, *Woodsong,* p. 29.

9. Ibid., p. 24.

10. Ibid., p. 40.

11. Gary Paulsen, *My Life in Dog Years* (New York: Delacorte Press, 1998), p. 101.

12. Ibid., p. 116.

13. Gary Paulsen, *Puppies, Dogs, and Blue Northers: Reflections on Being Raised by a Pack of Sled Dogs* (San Diego, Calif.: Harcourt Brace, 1996), p. 45.

14. Alice Cary, *BookPage,* March 1994, p. 18.

15. Paulsen, *Puppies, Dogs, and Blue Northers,* p. 36.

16. *ABC World News,* Saturday, March 5, 1994.

17. "Gary Paulsen," *Something About the Author* (Detroit, Mich.: Gale Research Inc., 1989), vol. 54, p. 81.

18. *ABC World News,* Saturday, March 5, 1994.

Chapter 7. Dancing With Winter: The Iditarod

1. Rich Davis, "Dog Sleds and Iditarod Fuel Author's Sense of Adventure," *The Evansville* [Indiana] *Courier,* March 8, 1992, p. F1.

2. Gary Paulsen, *Winterdance: The Fine Madness of Running the Iditarod* (San Diego, Calif.: Harcourt Brace, 1994), p. 145.

3. Ibid.

4. Dorothy M. Broderick, ed., Young Adult Library Services Association, American Library Association, *A Printz of a Man, A Festschrift in Honor of Mike Printz* (Madison, Wisc.: Omni Press, 1997), p. 74.

5. Ibid.

6. Paulsen, *Winterdance*, p. 16.

7. Ibid., p. 14.

8. Jane Sumner, "On The Run," *Dallas Morning News*, April 18, 1994, p. 11C.

9. Gary Paulsen, speaking at a book signing at the White Rabbit Children's Books, La Jolla, Calif., May 5, 1999.

10. Davis, p. F5.

11. *Sunday Morning With Charles Kurault*, December 4, 1998.

12. Nancy Gibson, "A Survivor of Childhood," *The Columbus* [Ohio] *Dispatch*, November 8, 1994, p. x.

13. David Gale, "The Maximum Expression of Being Human," *School Library Journal*, June 1997, p. 27.

14. "Gary Paulsen," *Something About the Author* (Detroit, Mich.: Gale Research Inc., 1995), vol. 79, p. 165.

Chapter 8. *Hatchet!*

1. Gary Paulsen, acceptance speech for Margaret A. Edwards Award from the American Library Association, San Francisco, June 28, 1997.

2. Gary Paulsen, *Father Water, Mother Woods: Essays on Fishing and Hunting in the North Woods* (New York: Bantam Doubleday Dell Books for Young Readers, 1994), p. xiii.

3. "Author Dedicates Book to Hershey Class," *Hershey* [Pa.] *Chronicle*, October 7, 1987, p. 3.

4. "Author Dedicates Latest Book to Middle School Students," *Hershey Chronicle*, October 7, 1997, p. 3.

5. Alice Evans Handy, "An Interview with Gary Paulsen," *The Book Report*, May/June 1991, p. 29.

6. Letter from Bradbury editor-in-chief Barbara Lalicki to Mary Ann Achorn, January 14, 1988.

7. Rich Davis, "Dog Sleds and Iditarod Fuel Author's Sense of Adventure," *The Evansville* [Indiana] *Courier*, March 8, 1992, p. F5.

8. Jim Trelease, "Gary Paulsen: His First Survival Story Was His Own Childhood" <http: www.trelease-on-reading.com> (November 16, 1998). Used with permission of the author.

9. Letter from Bradbury editor-in-chief Barbara Lalicki to Mary Ann Achorn, January 14, 1988.

Chapter 9. More Risks, More Books

1. Kay Miller," Suddenly Fame and Fortune," *Star Tribune Sunday Magazine* (Minneapolis, Minn.), July 10, 1988, p. 12.

2. Ibid.

3. "Author Dedicates Book to Hershey Class," *Hershey* [Pa.] *Chronicle*, October 7, 1987, p. 3.

4. Dorothy M. Broderick, ed., Young Adult Library Services Association, American Library Association, A *Printz of a Man, A Festschrift in Honor of Mike Printz* (Madison, Wisc.: Omni Press, 1997), p. 74.

5. Rachel Buchholz, "My Life's Work: Author," *Boys' Life*, December 1995, p. 28.

6. Adam Grant, "Dog Life," *Scholastic Scope*, January 26, 1996, p. 17.

7. Gary Paulsen, *Winterdance: The Fine Madness of Running the Iditarod* (San Diego, Calif.: Harcourt Brace, 1994), p. 256.

8. Alice Evans Handy, "An Interview with Gary Paulsen," *The Book Report*, May/June 1991, p. 29.

9. Broderick, p. 32.

10. Ibid.

11. Gary Paulsen, speaking at a book signing at the White Rabbit Children's Books, La Jolla, Calif., May 5, 1999.

12. Gary Paulsen, *Pilgrimage on a Steel Ride* (New York: Harcourt Brace, 1997), p. 111.

13. Elizabeth Devereaux, "Gary Paulsen," *Publishers Weekly*, March 28, 1994, p. 71.

14. *Booknotes Teacher's Guide for Nightjohn* (New York: Bantam Doubleday Dell, April 1997), p. 2.

15. Ibid.

Chapter 10. The Fine Madness of Writing

1. *ABC World News*, Saturday, March 5, 1994.

2. Alice Cary, *BookPage*, March 1994, p. 18.

3. *World News*, ABC-TV, March 3, 1994.

4. Rachel Buchholz, "My Life's Work: Author," *Boys' Life*, December 1995, p. 53.

5. Sally Lodge, "Gary Paulsen Receives Ludington Award," *ABA Show Daily, Publishers Weekly*, May 30, 1994.

6. Ibid.

7. Randy Lewis, "He Owes It All to Librarians and Dogs," *The Los Angeles Times*, July 31, 1994, p. E6.

8. Mary Ann Grossmann, "Author Gary Paulsen Draws Upon His Own Wilderness Experiences," *St. Paul* [Minn.] *Pioneer Press*, March 1996, p. 9D.

9. Jean Patrick, "Paging Through Paulsen," *Kids Today*, January 28, 1996, p. 4.

10. Gary Paulsen, *Puppies, Dogs, and Blue Northers: Reflections on Being Raised by a Pack of Sled Dogs* (San Diego, Calif.: Harcourt Brace, 1996), p. 37.

11. Dorothy M. Broderick, ed., Young Adult Library Services Association, American Library Association, *A Printz of a Man, A Festschrift in Honor of Mike Printz* (Madison, Wisc.: Omni Press, 1997), p. 73.

12. Ibid., p. 75.

13. Gary Paulsen, *The Winter Room* (New York: Bantam Doubleday Dell, 1989), pp. 1–3.

14. Cheryl Bartky, "Write What You Are," *Writer's Digest*, July 1994, pp. 42–43.

15. Helen Vandersluis, Edwards Committee Chair, Margaret A. Edwards Award, Miami-Dade County [Fla.] Public Library System Flier, YALSA, June 28, 1997.

16. Jim Trelease, "Gary Paulsen: His First Survival Story Was His Own Childhood," <www.trelease-on-reading.com> (November 16, 1998). Used with permission of the author.

17. Deborah Kovacs and James Preller, "Meet the Authors and Illustrators," *Scholastic Reference Library*, vol. 1, New York: Scholastic, 1991, p. 127.

18. E-mail to the author from Wendy Lamb, Delacorte Press, January 4, 1999.

19. E-mail to the author from Jennifer Flannery, Flannery Literary, September 30, 1998.

20. Maureen Conlan, "A Writer With Stories to Fill Two Lifetimes," *Cincinnati* [Ohio] *Post*, April 15, 1995, p. 1B.

21. Elizabeth Devereaux, "Gary Paulsen," *Publishers Weekly*, March 28, 1994, p. 71.

22. Cheryl Bartky, "Write What You Are," *Writer's Digest*, July 1994, p. 44.

23. Patty Campbell, "The Survivor Roars," *Children's Book Review*, Spring 1996, p. 45.

24. Frances Bradburn, "Middle Books," *Wilson Library Bulletin*, January 1993, p. 88.

25. Nancy Gibson, "A Survivor of Childhood," *The Columbus* [Ohio] *Dispatch*, November 8, 1994.

26. Alice Evans Handy, "An Interview With Gary Paulsen," *The Book Report*, May/June 1991, p. 28.

27. Paulsen, *Puppies, Dogs, and Blue Northers*, p. 33.

28. "Kids on Paulsen," comments from letters to Gary Paulsen, courtesy of Jennifer Flannery, Flannery Literary.

29. Message posted on <bdd.com.bulletin.board> Internet site, September 22, 1998.

30. *Sunday Morning With Charles Kurault*, December 4, 1988.

Chapter 11. Gary Paulsen's Legacy

1. Rachel Buchholz, "My Life's Work: Author," *Boys' Life*, December 1995, p. 53.

2. Martin Arnold, "Find Stories Boys Will Read," *The New York Times*, October 15, 1998, p. E3.

3. David Gale, "The Maximum Expression of Being Human," *School Library Journal*, June 1997, p. 26.

4. Letter to the author from Theodore Taylor, April 27, 1998.

5. Alice Evans Handy, "An Interview With Gary Paulsen," *The Book Report*, May/June 1991, p. 31.

6. Gale, pp. 26–27.

7. Author interview with Wendy Lamb, Delacorte Press, March 13, 1998.

8. Alice Cary, *BookPage*, March 1994, p. 18.

9. Gale, p. 28.

10. Rich Davis, "Dog Sleds and Iditarod Fuel Author's Sense of Adventure," *The Evansville* [Indiana] *Courier*, March 8, 1992, p. F5.

Further Reading

Buchholz, Rachel. "My Life's Work: Author Gary Paulsen." *Boys' Life*, December 1995, p. 28.

Grant, Adam, "Dog Life." *Scholastic Scope*, January 26, 1996, p. 16.

Kovacs, Deborah and James Preller. "Meet the Authors and Illustrators." *Scholastic Reference Library*. New York: Scholastic, 1991, vol. 1, p. 127.

Paulsen, Gary. "A Heart for the Run." *Reader's Digest*, April 1997.

Peters, Stephanie True. *Gary Paulsen*. Santa Barbara, Calif.: Learning Works, 1999.

Salvner, Gary M. *Presenting Gary Paulsen*. New York: Twayne Publishers, 1996.

Internet Addresses

Visit Gary Paulsen's Random House home page to read a letter from the author, changed monthly, and learn more about his background and books.
<http://www.randomhouse.com/features/garypaulsen/>

Jim Trelease, author of The Read-Aloud Handbook and the world's biggest fan of readers and reading, writes about Gary Paulsen and the profound influence book reading had on his life.
<http://www.trelease-on-reading.com/paulsen.html>

Read about the Iditarod®, the Last Great Race®: the upcoming run, mushers, dogs and sledding, teacher information, and book lists, including six mushing- or dog-related books by Gary Paulsen.
<http://www.iditarod.com/>

Find information about Gary Paulsen's life and books; includes reviews and interview sources. Kay Vandergrift's site, from Rutgers University, emphasizes the importance of the literature connection in young people's lives.
<http://scils.rutgers.edu/special/kay/paulsen.html>

This Internet School Library Media Center site includes information on Gary Paulsen's life, lesson plans, and bibliography.
<http://falcon.jmu.edu/~ramseyil/paulsen.html>

Learn about Paulsen's receiving the Margaret A. Edwards Awards for lifetime contributions to young adult literature.
<http://www.ala.org/yalsa/edwards/paulsen.html>

Index